Supporting Young Survivors of Abuse

A  Publication

Author © Laurie Matthew
First Published 2001
by
Young Women's Centre
1 Victoria Road
Dundee
DD1 1EL

ISBN 0-9539961-2-3

Designed by DM Graphics
Printed and Bound in Scotland by
Woods of Perth Ltd

Contents

Other Related Issues

Parents and Carers

Information and Other Help

Resources and Exercises

Foreword

This book is 15 years overdue as far as I'm concerned.

Fifteen years ago, I had already been working in rape crisis, supporting adult survivors of rape and abuse for four years. Although there was precious little information around about how sexual violence affected adult women, there was some, and I at least had the advantage of being an adult woman myself. Then I found myself supporting two young women who attended a support group we were running, and found myself learning a whole new way of working. Although they were very different in character and in what they were dealing with, I also found lots of similarities.

For starters, they didn't seem to understand what chairs were for. Disregarding my carefully angled seating arrangement, they opted for the floor. After the first time I offered a cup of tea or coffee, they brought their own juice. They asked a lot more questions about me than I was used to from adult women. Once they got to know me a bit, they were generous with their comments about my appearance, my hairdos, and the clothes I was wearing. When I say generous, I don't necessarily mean complimentary...

They talked about horrendous episodes of abuse in small bursts, punctuated by lots of chat about their pals, their work, their anxieties about their weight/hair/appearance and their dreams about what life might be like when it stopped feeling so crap. They challenged all my assumptions about what people might want in the way of 'support'.

Since then I've supported more young women. They were all different, with different stories and different difficulties. But they had lots of things in common. They were young, and because of that, lots of things were different for them. They had fewer choices over basic things like where they lived or who they lived with. If they were still living with parents, they might have little privacy to make a phone call or attend a support session. Nowadays, of course, lots of young people have mobile phones. They just don't always have the money to use them!

If you think there's an overuse of the word 'different' in the last paragraph, you've spotted what it took me quite a long time to learn – young women are DIFFERENT from adult women. So supporting young women is bound to be DIFFERENT from supporting adults! It seems ridiculously obvious now.

The Young Women's Centre started life in recognition of that difference. Over the last seven years the Centre has grown rapidly, always in consultation with the young people who use the service. It works from the basic understanding that survivors of abuse, young and old, are the experts on their own lives, and that our role as supporters of survivors is to provide the kind of safe space and unconditional support that enables survivors to find their own answers. For the Young Women's Centre that means constantly checking in with young people about what will work for them. The result is a service which is a model of best practice in the delivery of 'user led' services, and a Centre which positively vibrates with the life and energy of the young people who use it and shape it. Young people are **the centre** of the Centre. They don't 'attend' it – they inhabit it. Their involvement is obvious from the minute you walk in the door – the colours are bright, the murals are dazzling and the music is, occasionally, deafening.

Organisations like the Young Women's Centre don't grow on trees. Mores the pity! Nor do they grow out of air. A lot of hard work by a lot of people has brought the Young Women's Centre to where it is today. As well as the current volunteers and paid workers, who do the core work of the Centre on a daily basis, there have been social work students who came on placements and couldn't leave; social work practice teachers who were cajoled onto the advisory group; a young woman who said she wanted to make a CD for the Centre and pressganged a local music producer into making it happen; a group of inmates from the local prison who painted the new premises ("ain't that a lovely colour?"); a group of Debenham's managers who painted one of the rooms as a teambuilding exercise – then raided their storeroom for furniture, curtains, kitchenware and some impressively fake plants; Bill, who builds shelves and brings donuts; the advisory group, including a police officer, a health promotion worker, a retired executive, a rabid feminist (travelling incognito) an education worker and a couple of senior social workers, as well as the aforementioned practice teachers; and many many more. Last but by no means least, there are the young people who use the service. They are without a doubt the Centre's best publicists; they tell their mates, and their mates tell **their** mates and the mates of the mates tell **their** mates that the Young Women's Centre is a place where people will listen to them and respect them and do what they can to help.

It's a long list, and you might notice something about it. These people are all very – DIFFERENT! So what makes it possible for such a diverse group of people to work together so effectively? The answer lies in the vision that has been held by Laurie Matthew for many years and which (though she'll be mortified at me saying it) she has a talent for communicating to other people. Her vision is both simple and huge – an end to the abuse of children and young people. On the way to realising that vision, she believes that every single one of us can play a part in helping children and young people to escape from abuse, and heal from it. And she will use every available means to encourage us to believe that with her.

This book (yes, I am, finally, going to come back to the book...) is her latest attempt. What can I say? This book is – DIFFERENT! People who are busy 'doing' the work of supporting survivors don't often make the time to write down what they have learned from their doings. I am very pleased that Laurie finally got round to writing down the cumulative experience of the Young Women's Centre, and that the approach the Centre has developed to supporting young survivors can now be promoted more widely. And I was dead chuffed when I got Laurie's e-mail asking me to write this Foreword. However, her approach to spelling is legendary, and what she actually asked me to do was write a Fourword....so here it is:

BUY THIS
BOOK NOW!

Lily Greenan
August 2001

Acknowledgements

This book would never have been written if it were not for the courage of countless survivors in speaking out about abuse and the many dedicated volunteers who listen to them. Thank you!

Thanks to Anne, Marley and Nicole for sorting my creative spelling and grammar.

Thank you Bill for your rigorous proof reading despite finding the subject so distasteful.

Lily turned my chaos into order and made this book readable. Thank you!

Thanks also to Harry and Denise for going that extra mile with me and remaining patient and supportive in spite of my increasingly unrealistic demands.

Laurie Matthew
September 2001

Setting
the Scene

This book is the result of seven years of experience of working with young survivors gained in the Young Women's Centre and ten years of working with survivors in rape crisis. It is intended to raise awareness and assist people who come in contact with young survivors of abuse to be better equipped to understand the many issues involved and provide meaningful support.

Many people are understandably reluctant to begin the process of supporting young survivors, as they fear they will get things wrong and make matters worse for the young person. Unfortunately, this can leave the young person feeling very alone and isolated as the adults in their lives seek out the experts who can help. While expert help is a great bonus for a young survivor and often very necessary, ordinary people including parents, carers and workers in different agencies can do a great deal to help young people and can work alongside counsellors, therapists and professionals to provide a whole network of support.

This book is aimed at workers, parents, carers, friends, family and indeed anyone else who wishes to understand young survivors better and be part of the network of support that young survivors of abuse deserve. The book is written in layman's language to make it as accessible as possible to all who wish to make use of it. While it cannot possibly cover every aspect or issue of abuse that young people have to deal with, we have attempted to cover as many of the most common issues as possible. Hopefully this book will encourage people to read further on the subject and increase their own knowledge and understanding.

Rights of
Young People

Under the UN Convention on the Rights of the Child and the Children's Act in this country, young people do have certain rights in law. It is common though for young people not to know what rights they have and even more common for people to deny them their rights.

The following list is some of the rights that we feel young people should be informed about.

→ Young people have the right not be assaulted or abused in any way, be it emotionally, physically, verbally or sexually.

→ Young people have the right not to be blamed for any abuse that they experience.

→ Young people have the right to be safe and happy.

→ Young people have the right to information they need in order to make informed decisions that affect themselves.

→ Young people have the right to make their own decisions about their future.

→ Young people have the right to speak, be listened to and be believed in what they say.

→ Young people have the right to request and receive confidentiality in matters concerning themselves.

→ Young people have the right to be treated with respect and dignity.

→ Young people have the right to ask for and receive support and help from others.

→ Young people have the right to be offered support without having to ask for it.

→ Young people have the right to say No.

→ Young people have the right to be protected from harm.

→ Young people have the right to their own opinions, beliefs and values; and to have those respected.

→ Young people have the right not to be exploited in any way.

→ Young people have the right to complain and be taken seriously in their complaints.

→ Young people have the right to be kept informed of any proceedings taking place which directly involve them.

→ Young people have the right to express their feelings.

→ Young people have the right to equality and not to be discriminated against on any grounds whatsoever.

The Young
Women's Centre

In April 1994, the Young Women's Centre was launched. Initially, it had begun as a small project within the rape crisis centre as the need to provide a specific service for younger survivors of abuse had been identified. Soon after setting up the young women's service, the need was recognized by young survivors for it to become a separate and independent organisation. By 1997, the Young Women's Centre had separated from the rape crisis centre and secured autonomy in finance, charity status and premises and had, with the involvement of service users, developed numerous projects of it's own.

The Young Women's Centre is a voluntary organisation, which initially only provided support for young women aged 18 and under who had been sexually abused. We now work with males under 18 also. We offer a free and confidential service providing face to face support, telephone support, support groups, advocacy and befriending. The Centre has also developed abuse prevention materials aimed at all age groups.

One of the first aims of the Centre was to consult with young people to identify what form the service could take that would make it accessible to users. We consulted with over 200 young people in Dundee and identified several ways to make the service acceptable to young women. This consultation process has continued to keep in touch with the ever-changing needs of young people.

Many young survivors try to speak about their abuse, but frequently they meet with an unsupportive response. Family, friends or workers often react with disbelief, anger or fear, or rush to pass the problem onto someone else. Often the feelings of young survivors are lost, overlooked or disregarded in the wake of a disclosure. It takes tremendous courage for young people to break silence and begin to speak about abuse and it is important that the person they speak to has some awareness of how to respond supportively. It is also vital that the person be aware of all services that exist for young people.

The Young Women's Centre provides a free telephone helpline and long term, confidential, face-to-face support for young people. We also support parents and friends of young people who have been abused. We liaise with many other agencies and offer to support any young survivor who wishes to access those agencies.

This Centre allows young people the space they need, to speak, be heard, and be given the information that can help them make informed decisions as to their futures. Often we can act as an effective bridge, which allows young, vulnerable people to access some statutory agencies they might otherwise never consider. Many of these survivors have never come to the attention of statutory agencies and have never been able to speak about the abuse they suffered.

We are working towards ending abuse of women and children and one of the most important steps in achieving this is to encourage survivors to break silence. We see this as a vital first step towards empowerment and moving towards healing. We also hope that through early support, these young survivors will not develop many of the harmful coping mechanisms and problems that many adult survivors experience.

As well as supporting survivors and their families, we offer talks, training and workshops to youth groups, schools and voluntary and statutory agencies. We are involved in Cross Party groups and interagency training events and provide consultation on working with young survivors across Scotland. **We believe all agencies involved with young people need to work together to provide a network of services catering for the individual needs of the young survivor.**

Child Sexual Abuse

- Facts and Myths

Myth
Some children, especially girls, initiate a sexual relationship with the man.

Fact
This is quite untrue. Children do not initiate the acts of abuse. Even if this were true, all adults know that it is both morally and legally wrong to be involved sexually with any child. Children do not know about sexual activity unless they have been taught to be sexual. Children have a right to be hugged and loved in a safe and non-sexual way. Abusers, when caught, often blame the child.

Myth
Children sometimes tell lies about sexual abuse. They do so to get people into trouble and do not know the difference between fantasy and reality.

Fact
The most common lie that children tell about sexual abuse is that it is not happening at all even when it is. They frequently are afraid to tell the truth and often when they do try to tell, they are not believed. Sometimes, when they do tell, the reactions of the adults are so extreme that the children retract their story. It is very rare for a child to lie about being abused and children ought not to have the intimate knowledge required to describe an act of sexual activity.

Myth
Even though children may not like the sex, they often enjoy the attention they receive.

Fact
Sexual abuse is wrong. Children have a right to receive attention and love that is not abusive. They have a right to enjoy attention without the added unwanted attention of abuse. Some children crave attention quite simply because they are starved of affection and suffer from neglect. This does not excuse abusing them.

Myth

The partners of abusers nearly always have problems and difficulties in coping with life.

Fact

Anyone can have problems or difficulties in coping with life, but that is no reason or excuse to abuse children. It is not the partner's fault so long as he or she is not colluding with the abuser. Partners are usually the last to find out and rarely know about the abuse at the time. It is the abuser who is to blame.

Myth

If a child feels pleasure in an abusive relationship, then the effects are not so bad.

Fact

The human body is physically designed to feel pleasure and abusers often sexually stimulate children until their bodies react. The effects of the abuse will be just as bad if this has happened and often survivors of abuse feel that their body has betrayed them also.

Myth

People who sexually abuse children have usually been abused in their own childhood.

Fact

Most abusers are male and most of the abuse happens to females therefore this just doesn't add up. This is just another excuse that abusers use, when caught, to try and evade responsibility for their crimes against children. Adults have choices and if they abuse children, they have chosen to do so regardless of how they grew up. Anyone who has been abused knows how bad it feels and therefore knows the effects of their actions on children. The vast majority of abuse survivors are very protective of children as they are often more aware of the vulnerability of children.

Myth

What happens to a child when they disclose abuse is often worse than the abuse itself.

Fact

Much depends on the adults closest to the child. Children are often not believed. If they are, it is a difficult crime to prove. Often, the reactions of parents, family, friends and neighbours cause great distress to children who disclose abuse. Also, the legal and medical procedures are often very distressing for children. Sometimes, though, the only way out of abusive situations is for the child to tell. Children ought to be able to tell about abuse, get it to stop, receive support and get justice.

Myth
Mothers are often to blame for the abuse because they were not doing enough to satisfy their man's sexual urges.

Fact
Men do not abuse children because they are sexually frustrated. If they are frustrated, they could find a willing woman or they could masturbate. This myth is insulting to men in that it assumes them to be unable to control themselves sexually. This is yet another excuse, and an attempt to blame women for the actions of some men. Sexual abuse is abuse of power using sex as a weapon.

The Reality
of Abuse

Numerous children and young people grow up with the experience of violence and abuse. This is a bitter reality that many of us have to face in our personal and professional lives. Many people try to distance themselves from abuse and violence and think that they will never have to face up to it in their lives. Unfortunately, when abuse is disclosed, the effects are so far reaching that countless people's lives are touched by it.

The abuses that children and young people experience can range from physical abuse and neglect to rape, torture and death. No abuse of a child or young person can ever be classed as mild and though some children may or may not appear to suffer trauma as a result of the abuse at the time, this does not mean that they have not been affected by it. Though many young people manage to grow up apparently unaffected by their experiences, others throughout their lives experience a wide range of problems that can be traced back to the earlier traumatic experience.

More and more adults are now coming forward to disclose abuse that happened in their childhood and many report suffering from conditions such as depression, post-traumatic stress, drug and drink problems, anxiety and relationship problems. Many adult survivors also testify to receiving little or no support or help as children or young people while experiencing the abuse or even afterwards. For some this was clearly due to the fact that they never disclosed the abuse at the time, but for others who did, few are able to say that they were adequately supported during or after the disclosures.

It is difficult to know the true number of children who are abused in childhood as very few disclose the abuse until they reach adulthood. Even then, it can take many years before it all comes out. Research has been conducted to establish how widespread the problem is, but, in reality the true extent of child abuse will probably never be known to us.

The Young Women's Centre regularly consults with young people to find out what they need and want, to obtain their views and try to find out the scale of the problem. The following is a summary of one of our consultations carried out in November 2000.

Summary of Consultation Results
November 2000

We consulted with a total of 1072 young people.

50% of respondents were from Dundee and the rest from across Scotland. We tried to consult with equal numbers of males and females. Some young men we approached chose not to respond and therefore, 60% of respondents were female and 40% male. The consultation was aimed primarily at 12 - 18 year olds. 73.3% of the young people were aged between 13 and 16.

About one in five of those we consulted had heard about the Young Women's Centre but there were still many who had not. Those who knew of the Centre had heard about it in a number of ways but mostly from school, or from friends. Of those who had not heard about the Centre before, most felt that they would rather find out more about it from friends or leaflets.

Most of those consulted (82.7%) thought there was a definite need for a service like the Young Women's Centre in their area. 70% of the respondents felt they didn't know enough about sexual abuse and 53.5% felt that they should find out more about the issues in school.

Those consulted thought that it would be easier to speak about rape and sexual abuse to friends (41.3%), family (27.9%) or the Young Women's Centre (25.2%) rather than to statutory workers. The people they were least likely to talk to were teachers (5.8%). It was also thought that trust; confidentiality and being listened to were the most important factors in telling someone about sexual abuse (Many chose more than one response and saw telling about abuse as needing several factors combined).

We asked the young people some general questions. In reply to these: 68.7% felt it should be against the law to hit a child. Only 26.6% had heard of the UN Convention on the Rights of the Child, and of those who had not, 67.2% wanted to find out more about it. Only 17% of young people felt they were always protected from violence while 17% felt they were never protected from violence. 33% felt that violence was never justified. 83% felt they should have equal rights with adults; 44% felt they should get equal pay for equal work; 32% felt they should have the same degree of confidentiality as adults get; 76% felt someone should tell them their rights; 55.8% thought that they should learn this in school.

47% of the young people knew someone who had been abused; of those, 34.5% were female. The main types of abuse were physical (45.8%) and sexual (42.5%).

Roughly 1 in 4 of those who were prepared to answer the question (84.7% responded) told us they had been abused.

Young people indicated that most abuse happened to them in the street, at school or at home. 48.3% of the respondents said that they told about the abuse at the time. 68.5% said that they told someone later. The people they mostly told were their friends or their mum.

73.8% of the respondents said they would use the Young Women's Centre or would recommend it to a friend.

80.3% of respondents thought that the Young Women's Centre should support boys as well as girls.

This survey shows that amongst the young people consulted, there was a high degree of abuse and violence in their lives. Many knew of other young people who had been abused and 1 in 4 said that they had been abused themselves. This brief consultation indicates that the scale of the problem is probably more widespread than most people believe.

Sometimes it comes to the attention of parents, teachers, friends or others that a child or young person has been abused and they have to find ways of dealing with the disclosure. This may result in an investigation and/or a court case, other times things are dealt with differently. Occasionally, the child is not believed at the time, often there is not enough proof and rarely is anyone actually convicted for the abuse. Even when there is a conviction, sentencing is erratic and is not always the outcome that the survivor actually wanted. For many young survivors all they ever want is for the abuse to stop.

Often young survivors are denied support and counselling if the case is to go to court. This is generally due to fears that evidence will be contaminated. Whether or not this would be the case, surely the welfare of the child should be more important than a court case that might not even happen or have a positive outcome? Frequently it takes two years for a case to even reach the courtroom and all that time the child and carers have to manage without support.

Regardless of the outcome of a disclosure, the young person will need support. This is often the area that many adults struggle with as they have little or no knowledge of how to provide adequate support for the young survivor. Many adults shy away from this as they find abuse of young people so difficult to deal with themselves and have a tendency to look for 'the experts' to help and support the young person. Sadly, there are few experts in this field.

How the adults involved react at the time and what they do during a disclosure and its aftermath are extremely important to the young person and can either help the young survivor towards further disclosure and recovery from trauma or can cause further trauma or even retraction of the disclosure. The impact of this on the young survivor can be tremendous, overwhelming and the effects can be carried well into adult life.

This book is intended to share with supportive adults the Young Women's Centre's experience of working with young survivors of abuse. It's aim is to try and equip adults more fully with the knowledge and skills they need to support young survivors in moving towards healing. Society has already failed young survivors instead of safeguarding them from harm. They deserve the best we can give them to minimise long-term damage and give them the best chance possible in life.

Adults **can** overcome their fears, cope with hearing about abuse and **can** help young survivors a lot.

The Politics
of Abuse

Few people ever think of the politics involved in child abuse and violence. Yet they wonder at the causes, carry out empirical research with survivors and offenders, and make many attempts to get to the root of what is really going on in a society that seems to permit violence to flourish. While it is important to study individual

cases and vital to provide support for those who have been abused, it is also necessary to take a step back from the individuals and look at what is really happening in society.

Our society is still dominated by a male perspective. It is strongly patriarchal and is still, despite attempts in law to create equality between males and females, very unequal. Men still firmly hold most of the power. Men hold the top positions in the fabric of society including Government, business, commerce, health, education, social work and law. Men are essentially the decision makers and control the wealth, education and health of this society. If we look at any hierarchical system such as, for example, the health system, we find that women dominate such areas as direct care of individuals, office administration and cleaning - the higher up and subsequently higher paid positions are firmly dominated by men. Despite the fact that over the past few decades there have been signs of change, still there is a huge imbalance in power.

It was the feminist movement that began to highlight the inequalities in society and a long hard fought battle forced some change as the men reluctantly gave way. Though this battle is not yet over, much of the early momentum has been lost and the tide has turned so much that to confess to being a feminist is nearly as bad as confessing to being a survivor. Myths and fabrications abound and have led some to believe that the feminist movement is either no longer needed or has died in the wastelands of cultural rejection.

The feminist movement in the 1960s stimulated and encouraged the survivors' movement. Whilst the abuses of women and children had always been an integral part of society it had never before been recognized as widespread or treated with any seriousness as something that should occupy the attention of society. What went on behind the closed doors of a man's 'castle' was his concern. Feminism opened those doors and they have remained open ever since, despite the attempts of the backlash to close them again by introducing such concepts as false memory syndrome, women and children as liars, vindictiveness of women in custody battles and myths about survivors of abuse.

On the back of the wave of feminism, women, realising that a window of opportunity had opened for them, began to come together and create the much-needed services for survivors of abuse. Women's Aid and Rape Crisis groups began to spring up and women supporting women brought survivors of rape, domestic violence and childhood abuse together. It is interesting to note how, as more and more survivors came forward for help, professionals finally noticed that there was a problem to address. What has grown out of this has been a wave of theories, medical models, therapists and experts in the field of abuse.

When the survivors' movement became unstoppable, patriarchy had to find a way to own it and gain from it. Survivors are now often regarded by the system as damaged, are labelled under arbitrary categories of mental illness and generally regarded as victims who are in need of treatment. There are now many therapists, counsellors and professional experts where before there were none working in the field of abuse and while they can often provide very valuable help for some survivors, not all survivors need this or can even access these people.

It is interesting to compare the strong and assertive male image that is still culturally accepted as the protectors of helpless and passive women, with the patriarchal system that medicalizes abuse and categorise survivors as in need of care and treatment. Yet, the model of women helping other women has been proven to work and be of value and continues to work. There is no denying that some survivors may need more specialised help, but before survivors were encouraged to see themselves as in need of counselling and professional help from experts, most of them got on with the job of living their lives.

The patriarchal culture dictates the way that boys and girls are socialised and still considers males as in some way superior to females. They are still the bosses, the experts and the heads of the household. As everything has been set up to suit the males in society, the only way women can fully compete is to behave in the same manner as the males.

More resources in society go to males; from the boys who by virtue of their disruptive behaviour in the classroom grab all the time and attention, to the abusers, usually male, who command the bulk of the available resources from criminal justice, police and prison services. Meanwhile services for survivors are still few and far between.

At the end of the day, males hold the power in society and the home. They are taught from an early age to be aggressive and superior. They are encouraged through pornography and newspapers to see women as sexual objects and socialised into believing that women exist to serve them. Women are encouraged to accept their passive inferior role as carers, homemakers and servants of men. All this works fine until some men overstep the slender boundaries of social acceptability and abuse their positions of power. It is little wonder that most abusers are male and most of the victims are women and children. Women and children are commonly seen as his property to do with, as he wants.

Until there is true equality in this society abuse will continue unabated. Until children and young people are viewed as individuals rather than as the possessions of their parents, abuse will continue unabated. Only by tackling the root of the problem will there ever be real and meaningful change.

The Cycle
of Abuse

It is common to hear people talk about the cycle of abuse, which suggests that if someone has grown up with violence and abuse then they are more likely be violent and abusive and to perpetuate the cycle. This implies that survivors of abuse are more likely to grow up and become abusers than those who have not been abused. It implies that someone growing up with violence will react to situations with violence in their adult lives. While we are certain that this theory comes from a piece of very valuable empirical research, it is definitely not our experience of survivors.

Having worked with countless survivors of physical and sexual violence for many years, we have rarely come across a survivor who fits this theory. The majority of survivors that we have worked with have been passionate about protecting children from harm. They have rarely been people who would ever consider using violence against another person, even to defend themselves. Yet, survivors have to live daily with the stigma of being labelled a survivor and judged under this theory. This theory is still taught in many professions and is widely held. It supports the view that, 'they don't know any different.' But survivors do know what is right and wrong by the time they become adults. They also know what it feels like to be abused and most would never wish such a thing upon another human being, let alone a child.

Unfortunately the many male offenders who after lengthy court cases and being found guilty of abuse then claim that they were abused as children, supports the theory of the cycle of abuse. Increasing numbers of these men, who have usually forced children to appear in court against them at great cost, suddenly declare themselves to be survivors of terrible abuse and deprivation. The fact that few if any of these men have ever disclosed this before being caught and found guilty seems to be overlooked as is the fact that they never reported the supposed crimes against them or sought any help.

While some younger children might well act out sexually or react violently if they have been abused, as they grow older they do learn what is appropriate and acceptable in society and the vast majority do not grow up to be violent.

Many, many people grow up with abuse and deprivation and could never consider hurting a child. What most have learned in growing up is not how to be violent themselves but rather how to accept violence and abuse against themselves. It is much more likely to be the case that a survivor of abuse will be repeatedly abused throughout their lives rather than turn into an abuser. Re-victimisation is, in our experience, much more likely unless the survivor learns how to assert their right to say 'no' to others.

Re-victimisation

Children who are abused repeatedly throughout their childhood learn how to find ways of coping with being abused. This can be much more familiar to them than living without abuse. By being abused, they often lose self-worth, confidence and any sense of self or rights. The abuser brainwashes the child into accepting the violence against them. It becomes a way of life.

Young survivors are repeatedly taught that they must obey the abuser and all their resistance is gradually broken down. These young people have a much higher tolerance of acts done to them by others and a much higher degree of acceptance of other people's rights over their own. Often they do not even think that what happened to them was wrong, as they believe that they deserved it in some way. Yet, in our experience, these same young survivors will go to great extremes to safeguard other children and young people from the same fate. We find that the young survivors who end up going forward to report what has happened to them usually do so to safeguard a sibling or another child.

It is remarkably easy for abusers to spot young survivors of abuse as vulnerable to their approaches and we find that many survivors are repeatedly abused, as they do not have the necessary skills to resist and are less likely to tell a second time. This is particularly the case when a first disclosure has either not been believed or has been dealt with badly by the adults. It is common for young survivors to be bullied by other children too as they find it so hard to stand up for themselves.

This pattern of being bullied can sometimes be taken into adult life. Many survivors of abuse grow up and become victims of employers bullying at work and end up repeatedly in violent relationships. None of this is their fault but it can be very difficult for survivors to learn to stand up to others. Abusers always seem to have the skills to find the survivors who are more vulnerable. Perhaps it would be useful to find out how the abusers can recognise vulnerable young people so that the people who want to help survivors can learn the same skills.

With early intervention and support, the young survivor can become strong and assertive enough to break this pattern of behaviour and many survivors do it for themselves. It is not inevitable that any pattern be continued with a survivor. Most of them are strong and adaptable people who have managed to cope with things in childhood that many people would find impossible to deal with as adults. It is best that they don't have to cope alone and that they can find someone to support them on their healing journey.

Excuses

Abusers make many excuses for their behaviour when they are finally caught. Few ever own up until they are caught and even fewer ever seek help unless it is thought by them to be a way of escaping prison or reducing the time spent there. Practically all of the excuses boil down to blaming women and children for their behaviour rather than taking full responsibility for it.

➢ **She was asking for it.** This is common and ranges from the clothes she was wearing which enticed him too much so that he lost control, or she was nagging.

How these can ever be reasons for rape, domestic violence or raping a child is beyond our comprehension.

➤ **He couldn't resist her:** This tends to be about how lovely she was and how he believes she really wanted it. 'It' being to be sexually assaulted by him. He of course couldn't help the fact that she was so beautiful even if she was a child.

➤ **It's his right:** He really believes that he has the right to do as he pleases to his wife, daughter or son. It could be his belief that it is the natural order, or a warped religious belief; either way, he takes what he wants.

➤ **She came on to him:** She was, in his opinion, acting in a seductive manner, which indicated that she wanted sex with him. Again, they can even say this about children.

➤ **They need to be kept in their place:** It's natural for men to control and dominate their women and children. If they would only behave and do as he says, he wouldn't have to be so firm with them.

➤ **He was only showing love and affection:** This is his way of showing how much he loves the person.

➤ **The cycle of violence:** He was abused himself and therefore either didn't know the difference between right and wrong or his reactions are so set by his childhood that he can act no other way. The 'cycle of violence' theory lets him very nicely off the hook.

➤ **He is sick:** There are many people who suffer physical and mental ill health who do not go around abusing others. With this excuse society seeks to distance itself from the abuser and his behaviour. People do not like to accept that the abuser may be as 'normal' as they are.

➢ **He's a paedophile:** The media have hyped up this word so much now that nearly everyone uses it. The word actually means 'lover of children' and again is used to create almost a separate category of people who cannot help what they do. Any person given this title is an abuser and he will certainly appear to be as normal as anyone else, except for the fact that he chooses to abuse children. Use of the word to describe an abuser safely distances people from the bitter reality that any adult can make a choice and some choose to abuse children. There are many different ways of abusing a child and not all abusers can be made to fit the narrow and media defined category of a paedophile.

Strangely, with all these excuses and the many more that they make to absolve themselves of all responsibility, they always manage to cover up really well to the outside world. They silence the survivors and plan everything really well to prevent themselves getting caught.

Some abusers would have the world believe them to be out of touch with society's view of what's right and wrong and they attempt to excuse their behaviour in many creative ways. Yet they are all very skilled and clever at abusing children and covering up what they are doing. **If they really thought that what they were doing was okay, why did they have to hide it from the world?**

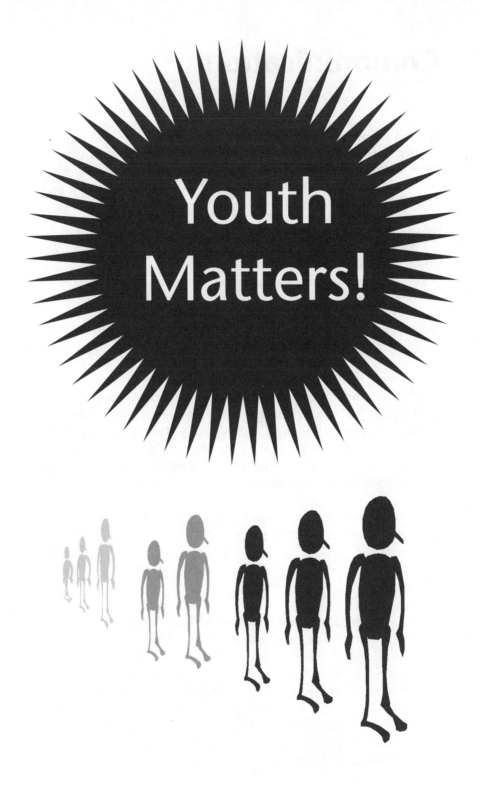

Communication

and Young People

We live within a culture where young people are seen to have little or no rights or self-determination, and are kept at a distance from the adult world. We have, as a society, developed neither the skills nor the inclination to communicate effectively with them. Many  adults constantly view young people with suspicion, intolerance and pre-judgement, if they even notice the young people at all. Many tend only to notice young people when they intrude into the adult world, and then they are treated as though they are a problem and have no right to be there.

Consider the signs on shop doors that say 'only two school children at a time'. Consider how often young people are harassed by the police on the streets, generally because some adults have complained about their presence. With any other group of people, these acts would, quite rightly, be seen, as discrimination and prejudice and pressure groups for equal rights would campaign against such injustices. Not so for young people though!

Sometimes, the only communication adults have had with a young person at all has been to tell them to "go away" or to "be quiet". In view of this, is it any wonder that young people sometimes get angry or frustrated, or remain silent in the presence of adults?

Communication with an adult can be extremely difficult for young people, particularly when it becomes obvious to them that adults don't want to listen, or have no interest in them personally or in what they have to say. As a society, we are highly prejudiced against young people and see our adult world as more important than the world of young people; dismissing the thoughts, feelings, opinions and activities of young people as, at best, cute or funny, but more usually as disruptive, an inconvenience, unimportant or silly.

If we hope to work with young people and support them, adults need to challenge their own attitudes and prejudice towards young people. It is important to remember that the only difference between young people and adults is that they are inexperienced in some things. Young people have not had the advantage of the years of experience that only time can bring, yet the experiences that some young survivors may have had, despite their youth, may be more than some adults may ever have had in their lives, or be able to cope with.

A young person who has been severely abused, raped or sexually assaulted will have the difficulty of communicating with an adult further intensified by the fact that the young person will have learned not to trust people, or indeed the world in general. The young person will possibly have no faith in the fact that they have a right to be listened to and understood in an alien and often-hostile adult world. If the young person has already been abused by an adult (which is the most likely case), then it may be much more difficult to talk to or trust another adult.

So how then do we tackle this? Firstly we would suggest that, as adults, we remember what it was really like to be young and get in touch with the child that we all once were. In doing so, we may begin to remember the feelings of injustice, frustration, anger, fear and hurt that often accompany even the most secure and loving childhood. Secondly, it is important to learn to respect young people as individuals, born with the same human rights as adults have. In respecting them, we need to question our whole way of speaking, or in many cases **not** speaking, with young people. Use of patronising language, put-downs, commands or demands need to be questioned and challenged in ourselves. We need to think about the tone we use when speaking with young people, we need to think about using their language rather than our own.

We also need, when attempting to communicate with young people, to be able to enter into their world. We need to adopt their language, enter into their play, be interested in their lives and activities and speak to them on their own level. It is too much to expect most young people to try and communicate on our terms. If this means sitting on the floor with them, playing in the sand pit, singing or dancing with them, drawing or painting, or listening to music with them, then this is what we must be prepared to do. Adults may even find it fun.

The most important requirement of all is that we must like young people. This may sound strange to some people, and they may even protest, *"Oh, but I love kids"*, but this is such a sweeping generalisation that it is almost rendered meaningless. It is not always possible to like all people.

Some adults will say, *"I don't know anything about young people"* as though they are some alien species they've never encountered before. If adults don't know young people, they need to ask themselves why not? It's not as though there aren't many young people around! Anyone who doesn't know young people has kept themselves apart and distanced themselves from them, possibly without even being aware of doing so.

Supporting younger survivors of rape and sexual abuse will be a bit different from supporting adults and for many will require a greater emotional strength. However, if as adults, we are prepared to open a line of communication with young people, we may give them the opportunity to recover from their abuse and get on with their lives. We may give them the opportunity to deal with their trauma earlier in life. We may help prevent the longer-term problems that many adult survivors experience throughout their lives. We may even find our own lives enriched by the experience of being allowed into the world of the young.

No one has to wait for an abused young person to come along in order to practise communication skills. Take a look around you - there are a lot of young people about now who you could begin to speak with and practise communication skills. You never know, you might even grow to like talking to young people. Young people are our future, and we **must** invest in them.

Discrimination

Young people suffer from discrimination just by virtue of being young. The discrimination they experience takes many shapes and forms. Though young people do have rights, they are not often informed about what these rights actually are. Often too, even though they may know their rights, the adults in their lives, who believe that they know better what is needed, frequently disregard the rights and views of young people.

Young people have little or no say in where they live. Parents and carers generally make these decisions for them. While this is justifiable in most cases, as these adults are acting in the best interests of their children, there are exceptions. Some parents and carers neglect the needs of their children and some abuse them. In these cases, it is only if the abuse or lack of care comes to light and abuse is proven, that the children can be given help or allowed to live elsewhere. Unfortunately, abuse does not always come to light. These young people are then stuck in the situation of abuse. They have no right to choose not to live at home without providing good reason as to why they don't want to. This is part of the reason that young people run away from home and are forced to live rough.

Young people, even when they are old enough to work or get benefits, are not provided with the same wage or financial help as adults. They get less housing benefit, less income support and it is assumed that they have family to help them. While many do have family support, again, unfortunately, this is not always the case. Younger people have no legal means of getting enough money to survive. This is part of the reason that some young people are forced into crime, prostitution and pornography.

Young people are seen to be a problem by numerous adults. While some young people may be a problem, there are a great many who are young people with problems, rather than a problem in themselves. The attitudes that some adults have in regard to young people often creates a bigger problem. They are moved on, harassed by the police and seen as a nuisance. This only creates needless barriers between people.

Young people have no say in their education. They are usually forced into a system that dictates what and when they learn. Despite the fact that all this does is create a majority of young people who are so switched off to further education that they leave the education system as quickly as possible, adults persist in this. Though this system does suit some young people, it certainly does not suit most of them. Neither does the education they receive equip them for life in the adult world.

Young people are used to being patronised and disregarded by adults. They are also used to being treated as though they are thieves in shops as they are either not allowed in, or followed and watched by guards while in shops.

Young people are often denied access to contraception, as they are deemed too young. Then if a young woman gets pregnant, she is blamed. There is always the assumption made when a young woman becomes pregnant that she is in some way promiscuous. This is not always the case. There are some occasions when a young woman has been forced to have sexual intercourse. If she becomes pregnant as a result of this, she may be unable or unwilling to tell about the abuse that she has suffered. Even if abuse has not been the cause, the fact is that young people seldom wait until the age that adults consider sexual activity permissible before they experiment.

Because young people are denied their rights and are disregarded and patronised, there needs to be more consideration about how to address this. Changing this will take a very long time. In the meantime, adults who work with, and support, young people can address this in themselves and look at ways of challenging attitudes in other adults, and of empowering young people. Prejudice of any kind should never be allowed to flourish.

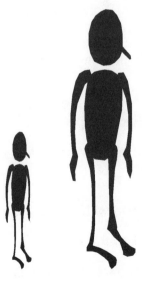

Child

Abuse

There are many ways in which a child can be abused. If a child is being sexually abused the chances are that there are other forms of abuse inter-linked with this, for example emotional and physical abuse. In most cases of child abuse the abuser is known to the child, and is in a position of trust or power. The abuser will more than likely be someone who appears to be an ordinary, respectable, well-liked person. Abusers are never obvious until they are caught. It is not only men who abuse children; women also abuse them (although in most cases that come to light the abuse has been perpetrated by a man).

Children, in general, are not in a position to stop the abuse. They may try to tell someone and be ignored, or they may not have the appropriate language to explain what is happening. The following lists may be distressing, may fill you with anger, disgust or helplessness, but they can give you an idea of what some young children have to go through. It may also help you to understand what might be involved when someone says they have been sexually abused.

Abuse Can Take Place:
→ In everyday situations, e.g. at home, in school or outside the home.

→ With or without being clothed.

→ As part of a wider range of physical or emotional abuse.

→ In an organised group setting.

→ In the presence of other children or adults.

Physical abuse
→ Hitting the child with hands, fists or an object.

→ Shaking or kicking the child.

→ Dislocating or fracturing the child's bones.

→ Burning the child.

→ Wounding the child.

→ Strangling the child.

→ Drowning the child.

Neglect

→ Leaving a child unattended for long periods of time.

→ Not getting medical attention for the child when ill.

→ Allowing the child to be in danger e.g. not guarding a fire.

→ Not catering for basic needs i.e. inadequate heat, clothing, food or drink.

→ Ignoring the child when the child is in distress.

→ Lack of hygiene e.g. not changing a baby's nappy when required.

→ Disregarding needs such as education, socialisation, etc.

Sexual Abuse can be:

→ Watching the child in an intrusive or sexual way as they bathe, use the toilet or while getting dressed or undressed.

→ Exposing genitals to the child.

→ Making the child undress and expose their genitals.

→ Rubbing sexually against the child.

→ Masturbating in front of the child or making the child masturbate.

→ Fondling the child and touching sexually.

→ Oral, anal or vaginal penetration by fingers, objects or penis.

→ Using weapons, e.g., gun, sword, glass bottle, knife to penetrate the child.

→ Involving the child in sexual games.

→ Taking sexual photographs or videos of the child.

Involvement of others

→ Forcing the child to watch a sexual act.

→ Forcing the child to be involved in sexual activities with another child.

→ The child is offered for sexual purposes by the abuser to friends and relatives.

→ Forcing the child to become a child prostitute.

→ Forcing the child to be involved in sexual activity with an animal.

Other forms of abuse

→ Depriving the child of food and water.

→ Locking the child up in a cupboard, attic or other small space.

→ Depriving the child of items necessary for their physical health, e.g., inhaler for asthma, hearing aid, and glasses.

→ Not allowing the child to sleep.

→ Tying the child up.

→ Forcing the child to smoke or to drink a quantity of alcohol.

→ Using objects such as masks or weapons to frighten the child.

→ Carrying out unnecessary medical procedures on the child.

→ Hurting the child's pets in front of the child.

→ Using treasured possessions of the child in the abuse.

→ Giving presents, which are then withdrawn or destroyed.

→ Forcing the child to be involved in ritual abuse or systematic torture.

This list could go on and on and still not describe fully the many acts of abuse that young people may have to endure. Abusers can, and do, resort to any thing. They are very imaginative in thinking of new ways of abusing children.

Though sexual and physical abuse are occasionally picked up and dealt with by the adults in young people's lives, emotional abuse and neglect, which can be equally damaging and life threatening to young people is very much the Cinderella of abuse. Even when neglect is revealed, it is seldom responded to in a manner that helps the young person. Hopefully, this will change in the future, as more people realise just how damaging it can be for the young people.

Abuse and Power

All abuse of children and young people is an abuse of power and it always involves some careful planning on the part of the abusers. Even in the more rare cases of a stranger abusing a child, it is carefully planned with a view to protecting the abuser from getting caught. However, most abuse of children and young people happens at the hands of a person known to, and trusted, by the young person.

The abusers often spend a great deal of time building a relationship with the child before beginning the process of grooming and preparing the child for abuse. The abusers need secrecy and silence to protect themselves from discovery. They also need compliance and control over their victim. Abusers are very skilled at choosing a child they can easily abuse. At the end of the day though, it is possible to break down the resistance of anyone if the right tactics are used. Abusers are very clever about achieving this.

Grooming Tactics

Some of the brainwashing techniques used by abusers to control their victims are extreme but not uncommon. While some abusers may use them in a disciplined and regular manner, others may use them sporadically. But even mild and occasional use of brainwashing techniques are often effective in gaining power and control. When they are combined with physical and sexual abuse they are reliable methods of keeping a young person silent and under control. These methods are not the only means of emotional abuse.

Most abusers who brainwash their victims use methods similar to those of prison guards, who recognise that physical control is never easily accomplished without the co-operation of the prisoner. The most effective way to gain that co-operation is through subversive manipulation of the mind and feelings of the victim, who then becomes a psychological, as well as a physical, prisoner. These methods form the core of emotional abuse.

Emotional Abuse

Sometimes a young person has rarely or never been physically or sexually assaulted but threats have kept them living in fear and caused them to gradually lose their sense of identity, as they have had to give in to the ideas and demands of a parent or carer. If the abuser has never hit or threatened the young person, but has used more subtle methods to manipulate, control and debilitate, the young person may feel even more confused and given to self-blame than many young people who have been severely beaten. A person who has bruises or a broken bone knows something has been done to them, but emotional abuse is sometimes so complex and bewildering it is difficult to name. If it cannot be identified clearly, the person it is directed towards may believe they are imagining it. More often, though, emotional abuse is not the only thing happening. It usually co-exists with other forms of abuse.

Brainwashing
used by Abusers

Method Used	Effects and Purposes
⚡ Isolation	Deprives the victim of all social support that would enable resistance. Makes the victim dependent upon the abuser
⚡ Disability/ Exhaustion	Weakens the mental and physical ability to resist
⚡ Degradation	Makes the cost of resistance appear more damaging to the self-esteem than capitulation
⚡ Threats	Cultivates anxiety and despair
⚡ Displays of total power	Suggests the futility of resistance
⚡ Enforcing trivial demands	Develops habits of compliance
⚡ Occasional indulgences for compliance	Provides some positive motivation
⚡ Distorted perspectives	Alters the image and perception of the victim in regard to self and in relation to others outside the family

Isolation

Isolation is the most effective way of setting the stage for brainwashing the young person. Once the victim is cut off from emotional supports and reality checks, the rest of the process is relatively easy. Young people who have experienced violence are often kept away from contact with almost everyone except the abuser, so that the self-interested, demeaning or threatening messages can saturate the senses.

An abuser often carries on a process of gradually weaning a young person away from everyone else they are close to through a combination of demands, threats and manipulation. The abuser may insult friends so they stay away from the home or the young person is too embarrassed to invite them again. The young person may be kept locked in the house. The abuser may keep the young person constantly beside them, except when at school. Even then, the abuser may prevent the young person from going to school sometimes for days at a time. The young person is then in trouble at school and the abuser may declare the young person a truant.

The young person may unwittingly collude in the abuser's campaign to isolate them because he or she is too depressed to want to be with other people or too ashamed to let others see them. The abuser may also threaten that if the young person talks to anyone they will be beaten or even killed.

The young person may not be allowed to see other people socially. They may not be allowed to speak of what happens behind the closed door, and the young person may be terrified of the abuser's violence or threats. To be on the safe side the young person may become unnaturally silent or superficial. The young person may become totally dependent on the abuser. Under such circumstances the young person is isolated from everyone.

Isolation deprives the victim of all social support that would enable them to resist the abuser. It also makes sure that the young person cannot talk to anyone about what is going on. It makes the young person dependent upon the abuser and more likely to be compliant. It leaves the young person emotionally and socially isolated.

Disability/ Exhaustion

A young person who suffers a disability is very vulnerable to all kinds of abuse. Tension, fear and continual rushing about in the effort to appease the abuser effectively enough to avoid any abuse wears out a young person who is subject to these techniques of brainwashing. It is also a huge strain to keep fear, sorrow and rage from showing to anyone. There may also be physical injuries to contend with. Enforced lack of sleep and/or an inability to sleep due to the stress can also add to the exhaustion. All these things leave a young person in this situation emotionally and physically drained.

Exhaustion weakens the mental and physical ability to resist the abuser. The young person gets quite literally too worn out to do anything other than try to survive. A massive amount of energy may be spent in trying to avoid further abuse and to meet or anticipate the abuser's demands, needs and expectations.

Degradation/ humiliation

This process of isolation and the self-doubt it creates are very effective in gaining power over another person. But there is more. The abuser may criticise the young person all the time both in public and in private. The abuser may continually say that the young person is bad, stupid and mad, or worse. Some abusers have extreme ways of degrading a victim such as forcing them to eat from a pet dish. The sense of extreme humiliation experienced makes the young person feel that she or he deserves to be treated as less than human and may cause them to think that no one but the abuser would ever care for or want them.

In addition to verbal insults, young people may also be physically and sexually degraded in quite severe ways. Degradation can range from refusing to allow a young person to go to the toilet and thus forcing them to wet themselves, or forcing them to perform extreme sexual acts.

All of this makes the cost of resistance appear to be more damaging to self-esteem than capitulation. A person with no self esteem at all, or low self esteem can believe that they are worth nothing and may see no point at all in resisting the abuser. By the same token, there would be no point in telling anyone or trying to get help if the young survivor thinks that they deserve nothing better.

Threats

Can be many and varied. The abuser may threaten to harm other children or members of the family. The abuser may threaten to destroy objects of sentimental value or pets. There may be threats about telling teachers or friends' things about the young person that will cause extreme embarrassment or humiliation. Emotionally abusive people can sometimes be incredibly imaginative in the threats that they think up to frighten and control others.

When abused in such ways, a young person's focus is on what can be done to preserve **short-term safety.** It distracts them from thinking about how to work towards gaining real security in the long term. Young people often do not have the life experience to differentiate between those threats, which are real, and those which are not. They often have no way of knowing what might really happen to them if the threat is carried out.

The use of threats cultivates feelings of anxiety and despair, which make it very difficult for the young person to think clearly. It also has the effect of distracting the young person from making any plans towards escaping from their situation.

Displays of Total Power

Abusers often persuade the young person that they are the ones who know the correct way that everything should be done. Usually the abuser claims to be superior intellectually, and to know the ways of the world. They often make sure that they hold all the power and exert a total control in the situation. They hold all the finance, withhold essentials such as medicine, food and drink. They exert physical control over all the victim's actions. Given that young people seldom have much control over a great many things in their lives, it is very easy for people who act abusively to take and hold control over them.

This total control over the young person suggests to them the futility of any resistance. Young people are relatively powerless and displays of absolute power prove to them that there is no point in trying to make any changes in their situation, as they could never win against the all-powerful abuser.

Trivial Demands

The abuser insists on the young person's compliance with trivial demands related to all facets of life: food, clothing, money, household arrangements and conversation. They monitor the young person's appearance, may insist on precise mealtimes with prescribed menus, which may change from day to day and be contradictory.

The young person may, for example, be allowed to wear only certain types of clothing. The abuser may suddenly change their mind on what is allowed. The abuser may make repeated demands for small things such as a glass of water, a newspaper from the nearby table, order the young person to pick up something that the abuser has dropped. Nothing becomes too trivial and the young person may be treated like a slave.

The young person often tries to anticipate the wishes of the abuser and thus deflect any anger or fallout. Everything becomes vitally important in terms of how it will affect the abuser. The thought and feelings of the young person are at best secondary, at worst totally insignificant.

The use of trivial demands develops the habit of compliance in the young person. They very quickly get used to carrying out any order or request that is made. Trying to please and pacify the abuser becomes completely automatic. The young person learns how insignificant their own needs and desires are and the control exerted over the young person is increased.

Occasional Indulgences

Abusers often totally confuse the young person by appearing to be very nice to them on occasions. These occasions are never predictable. They might give them gifts, sweets and treats and become very caring towards them. This gives the young person some hope that the abuser will change and quickly replaces the young person's fear or despair. Often the abuser gives the young person just what they are craving - love and attention. The young person cannot ever then see the abuser as all bad, as they have also seen the good side.

This provides positive motivation for compliance with the abuser. It cultivates the hope that the abuser will change and continue to be good. If the abuser then changes again, the young person might think that they caused it. Abusers often use this.

Distorted Perspectives

The abuser may manipulate the young person to begin to doubt his or her own judgment. Some abusers, for example may pick out a trait or physical attribute of the young person and use it against them. Traits can be exaggerated and distorted until the young person believes them. This may include things such as calling a well-built young person *'fatty'*, or a smaller person *'midget'*. Independence becomes selfishness or rejection and analytic ability is called *'coldness'* or *'showing off'*. When the young person begins to believe that virtues are flaws, their ability to make other judgments becomes impaired as well. It becomes increasingly difficult or dangerous to try and keep the situation in perspective. The young person may believe that the abuser has the right to abuse, may minimise what is happening and may see what is happening as normal.

All this alters the self-image and perceptions of the victim and his or her relation to others outside the situation. The young person loses a proper sense of identity and reality and is therefore less likely to be able to recognise what is happening or know what to do about it.

Possible Signs of Sexual Abuse

Unfortunately there is no simple way to know if a child is being sexually abused and many of the signs mentioned below can be caused by other things too. Probably the thing to be most aware of is a change from the normal behaviour of the child.

This often indicates that something is wrong though it will not indicate exactly what. At least noticing that something is wrong is a good start and adults can if they notice a problem begin to look for what might be causing the problem. The following list gives some ideas of what to look out for.

➢   Sudden onset of bed wetting.

➢   Refusal to speak, frozen watchfulness, hyper vigilance.

➢   Expressing dislike or fear of individuals or a situation.

➢   Unexplained injuries, discharge, infection, pain or irritation in vaginal / anal area.

➢   Excessive sexual knowledge for age.

➢   Use of sexually inappropriate language.

- Acting out sexually with other children.

- Acting sexually towards adults.

- 'Dirty' stories - may be their own experience.

- Symbolic play with animals or dolls, or themes in drawing.

- Becoming very withdrawn.

- Clinging to an adult or other child.

- Nightmares.

- Few or no friends.

- Fear of the dark.

- Hysterical fits or panic attacks.

- Running away from home.

- Depression.

- Over achieving/under achieving at school.

- Changeable moods.

- Being very unpredictable/violent.

- Being exceptionally good and well behaved.

- Sudden personality change.

- Outburst, tantrums, destructiveness.

- Self-harm.

More Vulnerable

Young People

Whereas all children and young people are vulnerable, some are even more vulnerable than others to abusers. Often these more vulnerable children are targeted for abuse by abusers and frequently the young people are unable to tell about abuse, but have to rely on the vigilance of good adults in their lives.

A child or young person who has limited understanding due to a medical condition is often bewildered by what is going on for them but may not know that what is happening is wrong or can be stopped. This would also make it very difficult to tell on the abuser. Such a child cannot always articulate or describe what happened to them. Some young people have a mental age, which is less than their chronological age and keeping them safe can be very difficult at times.

Children with physical problems may not be able to run away from abusers, may be unable to hear or talk, may be unable to describe what happened or may need help with intimate matters and become confused about the difference between abuse and appropriate physical help from an adult. All these young people are very dependant on the adults in their lives and many, even if they could tell, would be unable to due to fears about losing their carer.

Many young people in this situation are used to being controlled and even bullied by others. Other children can be very unkind to them about their differences and they are often picked on. This makes them an easy target for the abuser who offers affection and attention. The young person may not realise that the affection and attention is in any way abusive. Many of these young people are so used to being victims that they are incredibly vulnerable to becoming re-victimised by abusers.

Obviously the greater the physical or mental challenge faced by the young person, the greater their vulnerability and the greater the chances of an abuser being able to abuse them. Even less serious problems though can present young people with almost insurmountable difficulties.

A young person who cannot easily communicate would find it almost impossible to tell. A child who cannot hear or talk often finds their own way to communicate, but few people take the time to learn from them. This is compounded by the inability of the current system to take account of the communication difficulties and there is often no real or sustained attempt made to adequately listen to the young person.

A young person with little or no vision is sometimes unable to identify the abuser or describe the situation in a way that most adults can understand. Sighted people often fail to understand the ways of unsighted people and often unwittingly place many barriers in the path of telling. Young people who are visually impaired often have excellent memories, and rely on the other senses such as hearing or smell. Sighted people sometimes fail to understand this.

Few adults understand the particular needs of young people, and even fewer adults understand the specialised needs of young people with differences. The system of child protection that currently operates does not always suit these young people. Sometimes the person best able to communicate with the young person is the carer, yet frequently they are not listened to, or involved in the investigation. If the carer is the abuser, the young person is in an almost impossible situation.

All of these young people need adults to take particular care of them and stay alert to what is going on for them. Even people with extreme problems can find ways to communicate if the people around them take the time and are prepared to learn. Adults could also help by becoming more aware of the particular needs of different groups of people in society and the importance of communication with people on their own terms, rather than expecting them to deal with our terms and conditions.

Child Survivors
of Ritual Abuse

(This is an extract taken from our resource book on ritual abuse, **Who Dares Wins,** which is available from the Young Women's Centre).

Ritual abuse can be defined as organised sexual, physical, and psychological abuse, which can be systematic and sustained over a long period of time. It involves the use of rituals, with or without a belief system. It usually involves more than one person as abusers. Ritual abuse usually starts in early childhood and involves using patterns of learning and development to sustain the abuse and silence the abused.

Most sexual abuse of children is ritualised in some way. Abusers use repetition, routine and ritual to force children into the patterns of behaviour they require, to instil fear and ensure silence, thus protecting themselves from getting caught. Sexual abuse of a child is seldom a random act: it usually involves the abusers in thorough planning and preparation beforehand.

Some abusers organise themselves in groups to abuse children in a more formally ritualised way. Men and women in these groups can be abusers, with both sexes involved in all aspects of the abuse. Children are often forced to abuse other children. Pornography and prostitution are sometimes part of the abuse, as is the use of drugs, hypnotism and mind control. Some groups use complex rituals to terrify, silence and convince victims of the tremendous power of the abusers. The purpose is to gain and maintain power over the child in order to exploit. Some groups are so highly organised that they also have links internationally through the trade in child pornography, drugs and arms.

Some abusers organise themselves round a religion or faith, and the teaching and training of the children within this faith often takes the form of severe and sustained torture and abuse. Whether the adults within this type of group believe that what they are doing is, in some way, 'right' or not is immaterial to the child on the receiving end of the 'teachings' and abuse. Ritualised child sexual abuse is about abuse of power, control and secrecy.

There are occasions that adult survivors sometimes talk about, when if only the people they met had had enough awareness, it might have been possible for safe adults to notice them as children and perhaps have found a way to help them. Although it is very difficult for children to tell about the abuse, children can easily slip up and reveal a little of their lives. Adults with a raised awareness of the possibilities of what might happen to a child and prepared to keep an open mind, might just spot some of these children. Adults who take the time to build a strong relationship with a child stand a better chance of gaining the child's trust.

Children and young people living with ritual abuse in their lives do not have many of the choices that even other children have. Like other children they do not have access to information or money except through the adults in their lives. They will be well aware that police and social workers are not necessarily always safe people, particularly if they have ever run away. Also, professionals are frequently involved in groups and the children will believe that no one at all can be trusted. If they have been abused in a highly organised fashion, they will, understandably trust no one at all.

Children growing up with ritual abuse assume that it is normal and no one can tell them otherwise, as they do not know what these children are living. For these children, their life is normal and they have nothing else to compare it with. Children, being children, have to believe the adults in their lives, no matter what they say or do.

Children are totally dependant on the adults in their lives for all of their basic human needs. They usually love their parents, even if those parents are hurting and abusing them. They have, and are taught to have, great loyalty to their families. They also know beyond any doubt, and it will have been proven to them, what will happen to them if they betray their family by talking to outsiders. Unlike some abuse situations, in which the abuser threatens the child, children living with ritual abuse know that the threats are very real and will be carried out. They will have had this proved to them already.

As the children and young people will have been taught really well not to tell, it is unlikely that they will. Having said that, children tell in many different ways and there can be many signs that a child is being ritually abused. Children are not as good as adults at covering up, and the younger they are, the more likely it is that adults with good awareness can notice these children. The main problem at the moment is that safe adults completely fail to notice the signs that are there. In fairness to these adults, if ritual abuse is not considered a reality in our society, community or school, then no one can ever notice these children.

Things to Watch out for in Children who have been Ritually Abused

Being too good: Many young ritual abuse survivors are unusually well behaved and quiet. They are often so used to carrying out orders that this is applied to every situation and adult they encounter. They will do exactly as they are told, often in a very literal manner. They will not misbehave at all and will obey all orders without question. These children are usually not noticed by teachers because they are so good and quiet. They can often be regarded as model pupils, which indeed for the busy teacher, they are.

Non-socialised: Many young survivors do not know how to behave normally around other children. They may not know how to play naturally or join in playground games. Often they attentively watch other children to see how they are behaving. They may then try to copy so as to fit in and be 'normal'.

They may fear children's group games such as hide and seek, pass the parcel, etc. These games are often turned around by abusers and used to hurt the children. It is very confusing for children abused during a different version of 'pass the parcel' for example to find an adult suggesting playing it, and other children appearing to be happy and excited by the notion of playing this game. These children often do not actively or willingly join in such group games. They may appear fearful, uncertain and uncooperative. Sometimes these children are thought to be shy, withdrawn or even sullen. Some may act aggressively and disrupt the game to divert away from their fears and confusion.

Fear: Many things frighten children but with ritually abused children, there can often be a fear of things out of all proportion to 'normal' childhood fears. They may show fear of singing, circle time, paint, colours, making things, animals, stuffed toys, masks, religious items such as crosses or bibles, etc. Ritually abused children may show fear in a different way from other children. Rather than screaming, running away or crying, some children will freeze or even pass out with terror. They may hide in a corner or under a desk. They may repeat over and over again 'sorry' even when there is nothing going on that they ought to feel sorry about. Any unusual reaction to fear in a child should be noticed and gently explored further.

Running away: Most adult survivors report that as children they tried to run away on more than one occasion. Though severely punished for this, many kept on trying. Unfortunately, even on the occasions when police or social work become involved in a child running away from home, the real reasons for running away often remain hidden. Parents will pretend to be very worried about the young runaway and appear loving and concerned when they are returned home. Parents often lie about the child's behaviour, perhaps claiming that they are taking drugs, getting into bad associations, out of control or just rebelling.

Adults need to recognise that children and young people only run away from home for a reason, and there may be a very good reason for the children not telling the truth about why they have run away. The fact that police and social work continually return the children to the abusive home, in the eyes of the child, places them firmly on the side of the abusers. The abusers will almost certainly build on this by encouraging the child to believe that the police and social work are in cahoots with them and will always do as the abusers want. Understandably, these children will not readily turn to these agencies for help.

Language: Many ritually abused children know several other languages before they are school age. They are taught that they are not allowed to let outsiders know this. Sometimes though, young children find it difficult to hide what they really know and can slip up in using words or language that most children could not normally know. Also, ritually abused children may attach different meanings to words commonly used. They may have been taught that a simple word such as *'lemonade'* for example, means something entirely different from common usage of the word. They have no way of knowing that what other people call something can mean something different from their own experience of the word. Adults could occasionally check out what children mean and understand by some words. Adults could also question more any strange words or language used by children.

Touch: Ritually abused children often fear being touched. They are seldom used to okay hugs and the word 'hug' may hold a different meaning for them. If touched they may freeze, flinch, try to get away or not respond in a 'normal' child-like manner. They may appear to be afraid of touch or of touching others. Even a simple thing like being told to hold another child's hand may cause them difficulties and they often go to great lengths to avoid it.

Doctors, dentists and nurses: Ritually abused children are usually very afraid of these professionals. Parents will often keep the child away from school on days that these professionals visit. The children will find clever ways of avoiding seeing any of them and if forced to see them, will often react with extreme terror. They are frequently also very afraid of the equipment used by these professionals.

Behaving very badly: Some children living with ritual abuse may display very extreme behaviour. They may physically attack others, be very destructive, use extreme language, display hatred towards particular groups e.g. black people, women, etc. They may inflict torture on other children or animals. They may appear totally reckless with their own safety. They may well have been taught to behave in that manner, or they may have become unable to cope with their lives or unable to control themselves.

Drawing: Ritually abused children often find drawing difficult. They may not be allowed to draw or only allowed to draw some things as dictated by the abusers. They may be unable to use particular colours in drawings and will react strongly to suggestions of using a colour they are not allowed to or are afraid of. Textures of some drawing or painting materials may also cause them problems. Drawings are often misinterpreted by teachers or play leaders. e.g. a child may draw a cross the right way for them and an adult picks up the drawing and turns it around, assuming that the child has got it wrong. Adults could learn a lot just by asking the child about their drawings and exploring the use or lack of use of some colours or materials.

Making things: It is common for children in nursery and school to make things, especially at Christian festival times. Ritually abused children, particularly those from satanic groups, will find this very difficult as it is contrary to all they have been taught. Using some materials can cause problems for the child depending on their personal experience. Things like making Christmas, Halloween and Easter cards, for example, can make them physically ill. Again, ritually abused children may go to great lengths to avoid making some things and if asked to put particular designs or words on the cards, may be unable to do so. The behaviour of these children is sometimes seen as disruptive or uncooperative.

Places: Children may show extreme fear of particular places e.g. churches, cinemas, libraries, and graveyards. They may be unable to enter these places without being sick, passing out or becoming very distressed. They may fear some of the symbols associated with these places. They may also have difficulty with the people associated with these places e.g. ministers and dead people.

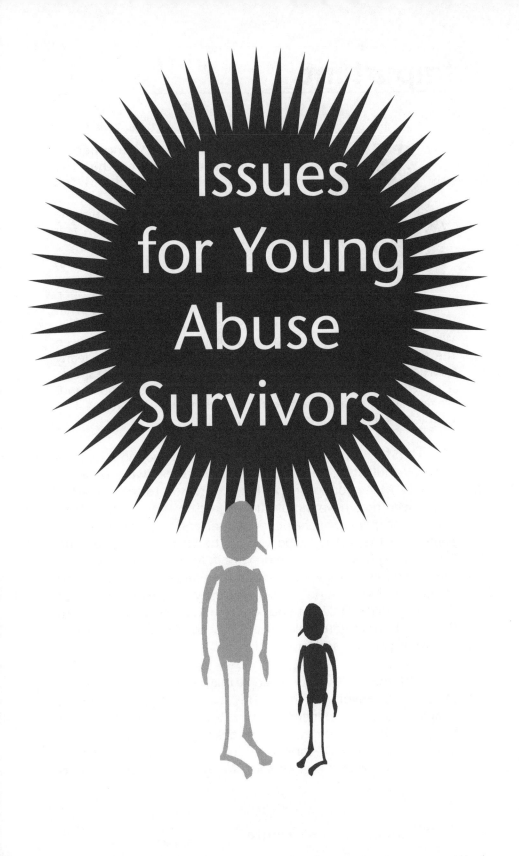

Issues
for Young
Abuse
Survivors

Important
Issues

Confidentiality - Young people need extra reassurance that the people they talk to will not tell anyone all about them. They may not have much experience of people keeping confidential, and often fear that their story will be spread to others. It is very important to be clear with young people what confidentiality you can offer, and what you cannot offer. It is vital that they understand what you are telling them, or they can feel let down and betrayed. Where there are things that cannot be kept in confidence between the supporter and the young person, this needs to be clearly explained to the young person preferably before they even speak. It is very important that they know exactly where you stand. Never make a promise regarding confidentiality that you will be unable to keep.

Trust - It may be very difficult for some young people to trust any adult at all; this may not be part of their own experience of adults. Many young people have no reason to trust an adult and indeed may have a multitude of reasons not to trust. Trust needs to be built up over a period of time and you may be tested. Sometimes the test is giving you a little bit of information and then waiting to see what you do with it. If you rush to pass it on, the young person may retract what they said or just stop talking to you. Getting a young survivor to trust you is seldom easy, but it is achievable by taking things gently and being very clear from the outset about your policies and procedures, if you have any, and what you can and cannot do.

Confidence - Young people may not have the confidence to approach anyone for help. This is especially true of young people who have experienced abuse. If you can show yourself to be approachable and clear in your dealings with young people, they can gain enough confidence to come and begin to talk to you. It is not always easy to spot the young person who lacks confidence. Lack of confidence can be easier to see in the quiet seemingly shy individual than in the young people, who act out, are in your face and loud. Some young people try to hide their lack of confidence behind an act of bravado and even aggression. Building confidence in young survivors is very closely linked to building the trust between yourself and them.

Testing - Young survivors are often more prone to test us and check us out before they begin to disclose abuse. Often they give a very small part of their story first to see how we react. It is very rare for young survivors to pour out the whole story right away. It is much more likely that they will test the waters first. Sometimes young people tell you a story about 'a friend' to see how you react to it, and at a later date confess to you that the friend is themselves. They may also test you in other ways. They may act out, behave aggressively, refuse to talk to you and generally test your boundaries to the limit. It is important that young survivors get a consistent and clear approach from you and you need to be very clear about your own boundaries and limitations. Being clear and consistent can help a young survivor feel safe with you and though the testing is rarely thought out or planned, it is effectively a way that young survivors can work out where they stand with you.

Ongoing abuse - We need to always be aware that young people are far more likely to still be in an ongoing abusive situation than an adult survivor. They will rarely let you know this at first, as they often fear the consequences of others finding out the whole story. It is almost impossible for a young person to succeed in getting out of an ongoing abusive situation by themselves, particularly when the abuse is happening at home. Often the only way this situation can be changed involves an investigation by police and social services followed by legal action. Many young people do not want this and fear it, so they are stuck in the situation.

This does not mean that it is impossible to intervene. It just means that it can be very difficult to persuade the young survivor to talk and help them to take action. With a young child, it is often easier and much more appropriate to take the whole thing out of their hands and report the abuse. This is often not the case with teenagers. Though it can be hard for the adults who are trying to help, it is better to take the time to build up trust, confidence and strength in a survivor and enable them to take control of the situation and get the help they need from others. Often the fears that many young people have of the child protection system can be alleviated by letting them know exactly what will happen if they go to the police or social services for help. Once they have more information they are more in control and much more likely to take action with your help.

Siblings - There is always the possibility of other young people in the family being abused if the abuse is within a family setting. There may be many worries about siblings that make it difficult for the young person to decide what to do for themselves. For the adult supporter too this can be a huge concern as they might want to give the young person time to build trust and take control, but have many fears for the safety of other children in a household. Many abusers keep control of survivors by telling them that if they do not maintain silence then the younger children will suffer. Survivors themselves often believe that they are protecting their siblings from the abuse. The reality is more usually that if the abuser is hurting one, he or she will carry on and abuse all of the children. Though this is a difficult situation to deal with, often it is the fear for siblings' safety that motivates young survivors to take action. It is never the responsibility of the young person to safeguard other children in the family. This is an adult responsibility and should be treated as such. While it is important not to guilt-trip survivors, it is also important to let them know that abusers rarely stop at one child. With gentle support and encouragement young survivors can take control of their situation.

Control - There may be fears of the young person losing control of the situation if he or she speaks out about the abuse, especially where some part of the abuse has already been disclosed and the aftermath of disclosure has been difficult. Young people who have been abused have already been overpowered and had all control stripped away from them by the abuser. They need to be allowed some control over their lives. Abuse of any kind evokes strong feelings of powerlessness and helplessness in any individual and part of disclosure and subsequent healing should involve the survivor in regaining their own power and realising that they are no longer helpless. Adult supporters can help a lot in this by giving

giving the young survivor control over talking, and what happens to what they talk about. All too often survivors are treated as though they are sources of information and witnesses rather than the very vulnerable people they are.

Family - There may be many fears around different family issues. There could be fears of causing the family to break up for example. Unfortunately, this can be a very well justified fear as different family members often take sides. Some may stand by the abuser and refuse to believe the survivor, and some may stand by the survivor. Whole families can be ripped apart by a disclosure, especially if a close family member or friend is the accused. There can be fears of upsetting family members by disclosing the abuse to those who love the abuser. There can be a strong fear around disclosing and ultimately being the cause of sending someone to prison. This may not be wanted as an outcome. Unfortunately, abusers often use many of these points to frighten and silence the survivor. Family is very important and even a bad family is often preferable to having no family or having a family breakdown.

Pressure - Young people live with strong peer pressure to conform. For some young survivors, conforming can be very difficult to achieve. When other young people are starting to go out and get into such things as discos, partying and relationships, survivors can find this very challenging. Often survivors are afraid of relationships, have a lack of confidence in new situations and generally feel that they are not normal. Some react by becoming withdrawn. Some react by throwing themselves into situations with no regard for consequences. Everyone is different in this, but survivors of abuse often experience real difficulties regardless of how they respond.

There may be the added pressure of exams, school and choosing a career, when the young people get into their teens. It is extremely difficult to think about exams while part of your mind is trying to cope with abuse.If a little bit of abuse has been disclosed, there may be a lot of pressure from adults to disclose further abuse.

Fears - Most survivors live with countless fears. There could be the fear of not being believed (they may have tried to tell before and not been listened to or believed). There can be the threats from the abuser, some real threats that are carried out when the young person steps out of line, or sometimes imagined fears which are no less real to the young survivor.

Female survivors live with the fear of pregnancy, and for some it becomes a reality. A young woman, who does become pregnant in an abusive relationship, may not be able to say how she got pregnant or who the father is. Assumptions are then made about her, which can be very distressing for her. Many survivors fear that they are or may become homosexual. This is especially the case where someone of the same gender has abused them. Young people who are on the brink of the very confusing period as they enter into sexual activity are often confused and testing out their sexuality. This can be even more confusing if they have been abused and learned to fear the opposite sex.

There may be fears that are very real to the inexperienced young person but not rooted in reality. This is especially the case for younger children. If they could only find a way to share those fears with an adult, it would be relatively easy to reassure them and help them see how unlikely the fear really was.

Language - Young people may not have the actual words to tell about abuse or may find difficulty in speaking about intimate matters. They may tell in a very different way from adults and adults may have difficulty understanding what the young person is trying to say to them. In young children sometimes saying they don't like someone can be their way of trying to tell. Even teenagers have this difficulty and many are telling in their own way through disruptive and violent behaviour, self-injury, running away from home or a multitude of other coping strategies. If the young person has been sexually abused, they already know that talking about private parts and sex is taboo and often find difficulty in finding the words to talk and tell someone what is going on. Young people may not understand that what has happened to them is actually abuse. They may love the abuser and be reluctant to betray him or her. Also they may have been receiving special attention, i.e. not being hit as much as other siblings.

Access - Young people may not know what services exist to help them and when they do they can find it difficult to get in touch with services. They may not know their rights or how to access help or advocacy. They may not have access to a phone they can use privately or even 20p to use a pay phone. They may not be allowed out of the home to even try to get help. Many services are not youth friendly and young people who have been abused often find it hard to approach a service for help.

Isolation - Because of limited life experiences young survivors sometimes think that abuse happens only to them. They can think that they deserve it and therefore would see no point in approaching anyone for help. Some survivors may not even know that what they are experiencing is abuse at all. They may have no way to know what is normal in a family setting, and assume that what happens to them, happens to all children. These survivors may feel very lonely or isolated even in a crowd.

Power - Young people may not know that they have any right to talk, say no to someone or seek help. They may feel completely powerless within themselves. If they have grown up in a controlled and restrictive regime where they have never known any sense of their own power, they may find it almost impossible to accept that they have any rights or the power to do anything for themselves.

Space - Young people may have no space of their own to think or work things out in. They may not be used to having space when they do eventually get it. Some young survivors may have nowhere at all that they feel safe or have ever felt safe.

Distance - Most adults are quite distant from young people and find it difficult to be on the same level as many young people. If adults are difficult to approach, patronising or superior then it becomes impossible for young people to speak to them or be properly heard by them.

Coping Mechanisms - The mechanisms that a young person sometimes uses in order to cope with a difficult situation may cause extreme difficulties. For example, the young person may be abusive, disruptive, violent, withdrawn, may forget what has happened, etc. These coping mechanisms can appear to adults to indicate a problem child, rather than a child with problems. The young person becomes labelled and ends up with a reputation, which further ostracises them. Frequently such young people are excluded from school and punished for their behaviour. A better approach might be to try and find out what the young person's problems are by building trust and confidence. Few young people who act out do so simply to give the adults a hard time.

Mixed Messages - Young people are not encouraged or taught to speak out about abuse, especially if it involves adults they know. They often need permission to speak about their experiences. They must be reassured that it is all right to tell and that they will be believed. They are too often taught to obey adults, to say no to strangers but not to say no to known adults. They are taught that they should do as adults tell them, without question, and are put down and ridiculed if they do not obey or give "cheek". Young people learn early in life that they are powerless in our society. In our society the message to young people is very negative. They may know that what has happened is wrong, and can sometimes feel that their silence had further implicated them in the abuse. Society does not encourage young people to talk about abuse.

Alternatives - The alternative to abuse for the young person can be an unknown quantity. The survivor may fear what might happen if it all comes out, and the abuser may go further, frightening or threatening the young person with actual harm. The young survivor may have no basis to know whether it will be worse or not, if he or she speaks out. It may even be that the survivor has attempted to speak before and the result of that disclosure has been very negative. Young people can sometimes not think of any alternatives and the terrible reality for them is that if they can't tell (and prove the abuse), there are few alternatives available to them.

Street
kids

Some young survivors are so afraid of everyone that they run away from home and live rough on the streets. Much as this appals caring adults and seems terribly risky, for these young people, the streets are safer than being at home. If they cannot trust anyone enough to approach them for help, they have to survive as best they can. These young people are very much at risk from abusers who might try to involve them in the prostitution and pornography industry. They survive in whatever way they can, by stealing, begging and sometimes selling their bodies.

These young survivors often live right under our noses in town centres, busy streets, parks, condemned buildings and anywhere else they can find a space. If you think you have come across one of these young people, you can help, providing you go gently. If you try to push things too fast by informing police or social services, it is unlikely you will relieve the problem. You may only be moving it, as even if they are returned home, they will probably run again, and this time they won't come near your area.

It is best to gently build a relationship and show the young person that you are someone to be trusted. Food will probably be very much appreciated by the young person, but you may well be met with great suspicion at first in offering it. If you go very slowly and try not to ask too many questions, but rather try to befriend the young person, you may be able to get them to the stage of trusting you enough for them to begin to tell you things about themselves. If they do, you have reached the testing period.

They may give you a little bit of information at first to see what you do with it. They will be prepared for you to betray their trust, and ready to run at this point. If you keep their trust, they will open up more to you. Some young people may be verbally aggressive towards you at first and they may test you in other ways. Be firm when it comes to money and possessions. They may well steal from you and try to play you for a sucker. If you stay fair, constant and non-threatening, you may break through their protective hard shell. Even if you fail completely to reach them, you have at least showed them that some adults care and can be trusted. **Perhaps they will trust the next person a bit more.**

Drugs & Alcohol

When young survivors are trying to cope with abuse, or struggling to come to terms with having been abused, they may turn to drugs, substances and/or alcohol to help them cope. Often their head is so full with the horrendous pictures of being abused or they feel so bad that they can't cope at all with life. Drink, drugs and substances that make them feel better, even for a few minutes can often seem to be the answer. Adults mostly know that these things will, in the longer-term only make things worse, but for the young survivor, they feel so bad that any break from it is a welcome relief for them.

The earlier that adult supporters find out that there is a problem of this sort, the better. Lecturing the young person does not always provide the best solution to the problem. The thing that can help the most is helping the young person to come to terms with the abuse, helping them cope with the memories, and standing by them. You can, at the same time, look for specialized agencies in your area to support the young person in looking at the new problem that has arisen.

Eating Problems

Some young people, for a variety of reasons can begin to develop problems round the issue of food. This can be a fairly common problem for young people who have experienced abuse. The young person may lose all interest in food, may obsess about food, may stop eating altogether, may overeat, may eat and then deliberately throw up; or any mixture of these.

On occasions, the type of abuse that the young person has experienced causes the eating problem. For example, if a young person has been orally abused, they may sometimes find it hard to manage the feel of certain kinds of food in their mouths. They may gag on some foods and may be flooded by intrusive thoughts or memories of the abuse when trying to eat. All this can be the beginning of developing a problem with eating.

Sometimes, the problem begins as an attempt to take control. The young person begins to believe that the only control they have over their lives is through what they put in their mouths, (or not), and therefore they begin to exert control over the quantities and kinds of food they eat. Over time, the control exerted gets tightened until the young person controls every morsel they put in their mouths. With some young people, they binge then force themselves to be sick to remove the food again.

Some young survivors start to use food as a form of comforting themselves. They begin to feel content only while they are eating and are therefore inclined to eat constantly whether they are hungry or not. Over time, this can become quite a problem for them.

Regardless of the way the problem starts or what form the problem begins to take, the young people who develop these problems need help to address it. They can be helped by encouraging them to talk about the problem, encouraging them to identify and talk about what the root of the problem is, and by encouraging them to seek help from their GP. A GP can refer them to a psychologist or other professional with experience of these particular problems.

Sex and Sexuality

Sometimes young people who have been sexually abused develop a problem round sex and sexuality. They can become confused about their sexual orientation, how they feel about their sexual identity, and how they respond to sexual contact. Often the problems begin to appear as the young person reaches puberty, and become more aware of themselves as sexual beings. Sometimes, the young person has, for the first time, discovered that the sexual contact they have experienced in their life was not normal.

Often, young survivors begin to think of all sexual contact as dirty or disgusting and become confused by the willingness of other young people to engage in these activities. Some can also become so confused by what the abuser did to them that they wonder if they are gay. Puberty is a difficult and confusing time for most young people and if this is further compounded by having been sexually abused, it adds to the difficulty. In addition to this, the young person may fear people of the same gender as their abuser and therefore have difficulties relating to them. If their sexual orientation is towards the feared gender, this can be very difficult to deal with.

Young people can be helped in dealing with these problems by being encouraged to talk frankly about them and being provided with access to information regarding sex and sexuality. Useful information can include sex education, access to support groups for people who want to discuss issues of sexuality and information regarding support agencies for dealing with the original abuse issues.

Sexualised
Behaviour

Some children and young people who have been sexually abused become very confused about touch, love, and sexuality. Sometimes the children become highly sexualised and begin to act out their experience on other children or behave in a sexually inappropriate manner with adults.

For these young people it is important to work with them to help them change this pattern of behaviour. A good starting place is often getting the matter onto the agenda with them. The young person may not even realise that what they are doing is inappropriate and if it is not brought out into the open it cannot be properly dealt with. In order to deal with this effectively, the young person must first realise that it is a problem for them and others and want to change the behaviour.

Adult helpers can often help young people observe and assess their own behaviour. Though the young person may believe that they are doing no wrong, it can usually be pointed out that there are consequences with such behaviour. Seldom is there no reaction to the sexualised behaviour of a young person. Taking a young person through the outcome for them when they behaved a particular way can begin to show them that something is wrong with it.

It may be difficult to get a young person to take responsibility for their actions, as they may not appear to care at first. There may be quite a show of bravado and aggression but often underlying that is a very frightened young person. While it is important not to blame the young person, they can gently be encouraged to see that what they are doing is harmful to others as well as themselves.

Some young people who have been abused simply do not know the normal rules of society and have to be re-educated in how they are expected to behave now. For some, this can be very painful as they begin to realise for the first time that what happened to them was not normal.

It can be a good idea to agree to set some goals with the young person, and begin by helping them to look at ways of decreasing the challenging behaviour, controlling the impulsive behaviour that might lead to their actions and helping them to be more in control of themselves.

Young people need to have an increased understanding of what unhealthy associations and beliefs, regarding sexuality, they have before they can begin to change these. They also need to have an understanding of natural and healthy sexuality, appropriate to their age and stage of development. A caring and supportive adult can help with this by raising these topics onto the agenda.

It is also beneficial to help a young person explore what love is and how to express that love in a normal manner. Young people who have been sexually abused by a person they love and who loved them in return, can be very confused by their feelings in this area. They may believe that it is normal to express all love in a sexual manner. Depending on the age and understanding of the young person such things as the purpose of sex and sexuality can be looked at and why people are sexual together.

It is important to talk to young people about their own rights, and the rights of other people in regard to their behaviour. They need to be encouraged to realise that they have the right to say no to other people in regards to sexual activity, and by the same token others have the right to say no to them without this being a rejection of them.

With young people it may be important to identify family patterns that sustain, increase or precipitate sexualised behaviour. While you may be working with the young person, much of the progress they make can be quickly undermined by their home situation, and may further confuse the young person. Often it is better if there are good links with the family, so that all are giving the same message to the young person.

Relationships

Young survivors can sometimes have difficulties getting into relationships, sustaining healthy relationships and coping with being in a relationship. Some survivors due to the abuse they have experienced, find it very difficult to say no to people and can find themselves in difficulties because of this. Also, sometimes survivors are easy to manipulate, easy to abuse and may carry forward many unresolved issues into their relationships.

With good support, young people can be helped to see that partner relationships are built on mutual equality and respect and sometimes have to be worked at by both parties. They can be helped to look at problems before they become too huge and can be helped to find solutions, which can lead to sustained and happy relationships.

Relationships with friends and family can often be difficult too as young people may have lost trust in the people in their lives. This trust can be rebuilt, and supporters can assist in helping the young people rebuild bridges between the safe people in their lives. Often young people feel let down by these people for not noticing the abuse, not believing at first or not keeping them safe. Sometimes the young survivor has taken out their feelings of anger and frustration on the non-abusive people in their lives simply because it was safe to do so. All this may have damaged relationships and supporters can help by assisting the parties in beginning to talk.

Criminal Behaviour

Some young people who have been abused turn to crime. They may do so for many reasons including; they just don't care anymore, they think that no one cares about them, they are angry with everybody or they want to get caught and get into trouble. Some young people are forced into criminal behaviour as a means of survival. For example they may steal to live when they don't get benefits, or may be forced by the abuser to carry out illegal acts.

Few young people respond to adults lecturing them and telling them how wrong their behaviour is. They respond better to support, good boundaries, showing that you care and talking through the consequences of their actions. Many young people don't think about how their actions have affected other people. When they talk about it and think about what they have done, they often express great sorrow at how their actions have affected others.

Pregnancy

Young women who have been abused often do not think about the possibility of pregnancy at first. If the abuse is revealed soon enough, the morning after pill can prevent it from happening. Unfortunately most young women are unable to tell anyone quickly enough and some become pregnant. When young women become pregnant as a result of being abused, they often try to hide it from those around them. If they are able to seek help, they can be advised about the various options open to them. They can go for a termination, have the child and allow it to be fostered or adopted or get help from family to cope with a child.

None of the available options are easy for a young woman to contemplate on top of the abuse. To further compound matters, few young women who have become pregnant will tell that it happened as a result of abuse, particularly if the abuser is a relative. Some young women are so inexperienced that they are not even aware that they are pregnant until they are very far on and thus their options are further reduced.

To help young women there are a number of things to consider. Firstly, if information and contraception is made available, an abused young woman can, if nothing else prevent pregnancy. Ideally, the young woman would be able to tell and get help to stop the abuse, but, if she is not yet ready to tell, at least she can protect herself a little.

All too often pregnant young women are judged by workers and agencies. If workers could only keep a more open mind and consider for even a moment that the young woman may not have consented, then perhaps the young woman will eventually be able to tell someone and get help.

The earlier the young woman can find out whether or not she is pregnant, the more options there will be open to her. While no termination is easy, the earlier it can be done, the better for her. Also, if she decides to have the child, the earlier she can get medical attention the better.

Young women can be helped to seek medical help and if they do not want to go to their GP, there are clinics that will provide a service without informing the GP. If the young woman is able to tell about the abuse and wishes a termination, try to bear in mind that the genetic make up of the foetus can provide valuable evidence of who has had intercourse with her. Many will not be interested in this, but some will if they are told about it. This evidence is definite proof in cases of incest and if she knows this, she might realise that she will now be believed if she wants to go forward to the police. Some might.

A young woman who chooses to have the child and keep it will need lots of additional support. The child will be a constant daily reminder of the abuse she experienced and she will need to be able to talk this through with someone she trusts.

This list is not exhaustive and all these may not always apply to any one young survivor. Every young person is a unique individual and should be treated as such.

Why Young Survivors
Might Not Tell

The real question here maybe ought to be 'why do they ever tell?' Telling is such a difficult thing to do and there are so many barriers to be overcome that it is a miracle that young survivors ever manage to do it at all. The main things that make it difficult for them in our experience are:

Not allowed to tell!

➤ They may have been taught from an early age not to talk about their home life.

➤ They might have been told by the abuser not to tell anyone about it - it's a secret!

➤ There may have been threats about what would happen if they ever said anything.

Limited Options

➤ Don't ever think about telling.

➤ Don't know that it is an option.

➤ Think that it is too late to tell anyone.

➤ Don't know how to tell.

➤ Think that there is no one to tell.

➤ Trust no one.

➤ No one asks or notices them.

➤ Have no words to describe what is happening.

Beliefs

➤ The abuse isn't wrong.

➤ No one would believe it.

➤ Things will be made much worse by telling.

- ➤ Believe in what the abuser has said.
- ➤ Adults are all the same.
- ➤ He or she deserved it.
- ➤ It's his or her fault it happened.
- ➤ Someone else would suffer if it all came out.
- ➤ Would be killed for telling.
- ➤ No point in telling, nothing would change.
- ➤ The abuse would get worse.

If Asked

- ➤ Would lie to protect self and family.
- ➤ Would deny abuse happened.
- ➤ Might tell in a way that no one picks up on.
- ➤ Has already told someone and not been believed.
- ➤ Thinks that they have been doing something wrong and will be blamed.

Other ways of Telling

- ➤ Not able to play or join in socially.
- ➤ Being a loner.
- ➤ Repeatedly running away from home.
- ➤ Extremes of reactions and inappropriate behaviour.
- ➤ Reactions not usual i.e. no reaction or overreaction.
- ➤ Mood swings.
- ➤ Living in a fantasy world.
- ➤ Sexualised play and behaviour.
- ➤ Drawing explicit pictures of the abuse.

Barriers:

A Young Person's Perspective

Adults often unwittingly create extra barriers, which prevent young survivors from telling and engaging with them. The following is a young survivor's view of the many adults around and how they behave towards young people.

Family:

- ➤ Will break up if you say anything about abuser.
- ➤ Will take the abuser's side against you.
- ➤ They love the abuser and you will just upset everyone.
- ➤ Will not believe you.
- ➤ Don't ever listen to you anyway.

Police:

- ➤ Always take you back home - back to the abuse.
- ➤ Call you a troublemaker.
- ➤ Talk about your poor parents being upset and worried in an attempt to make you feel guilty.
- ➤ Blame you for causing them trouble and try to make you feel guilty.
- ➤ Accuse you of wasting their time; say they've better and more important things to do.
- ➤ Believe your parents and any other adults.

- Don't even take the time to ask if there is anything wrong at home.
- Arrest you for wasting their time.
- Threaten you with all sorts of things.

Teachers:

- Add labels to you such as problem child.
- Call you sullen, arrogant, useless, aggressive, worthless, and stupid.
- Say you'll never amount to anything, they pity your parents,etc.
- Suspend you from school, give punishment exercises and never wonder why.
- Tell your parents about you and anything you say to them.
- Believe your parents ahead of you every time.

Doctors:

- Say it's a phase you're going through and you'll grow out of it in time.
- Threaten you with a shrink if you are acting out.
- Tell you to just grow up.
- Sometimes won't see you without your parents being there.
- Listen to your parents' explanation instead of yours.
- Just give you pills to control you and keep you quiet.

Neighbours

➤ Are too friendly with your parents.

➤ Believe your parents.

➤ Feel sorry for your parents.

➤ Tell on you at every opportunity.

Social workers

➤ Don't listen to you.

➤ Don't take enough time to really get to know you and expect you just to trust them because they are social workers.

➤ Want to keep the family together.

➤ See you as the problem, not the adults.

➤ Write notes about you.

➤ Think they know all about you because they've read the reports.

➤ Tell your parents things about you that you would rather they didn't know.

➤ Make decisions for you and about you 'in your best interest' without asking you.

Surviving and Coping
with Child Sexual Abuse

Survivors of sexual abuse are so often silenced that they have to employ many creative methods of coping to survive a situation from which they cannot escape. Many of these methods become so firmly established that they stay with survivors long after the abuse has stopped. Coping mechanisms can be seen as strengths - they can prevent the child from becoming completely overwhelmed by the abuse. They can help the child stay 'separate' and 'away' from the reality of the abuse, which may also help the child function in school and with friends. Coping mechanisms in childhood can pave the way for developing adult coping strategies.

Below is a list of coping mechanisms and stages of recovery that survivors may experience. It is important to note that this is not a checklist - individuals react and cope in different ways. An individual might exhibit any, all or none of these.

Forgetting

For many, the only option for surviving is to bury their experiences so deep in their mind that they actually forget that it ever happened to them at all. To someone that hasn't experienced this (and even for some that have) it seems quite incredible that something as horrific as sexual abuse can be blocked out so totally that it is completely forgotten. Some survivors may never remember the abuse, but whether the survivor remembers or not it can still have a devastating effect on their life. Sometimes 'life events' can trigger remembering, for example, the birth of a child, the death of the abuser, moving school, etc. It is not necessary for a survivor to remember all the abuse to deal with how they feel about it - some want to know exactly what happened, some don't.

Often children have to learn how to forget so that they can behave normally. They need to be able to adapt rapidly to many situations that adults would find difficult. As a result of this, they can learn to switch off the memory of being abused at night so that they can go to school the next day, act normally and learn in the classroom.

Denial

Sometimes survivors have memories of what happened to them, but because they are so painful or unbelievable to the survivor, the survivor denies to themself that anything really happened. If you don't admit that something has happened, then you don't have to deal with it. Denial, like all coping mechanisms, can help a young survivor cope with their life.

Minimising

Another way to cope with the experience of child sexual abuse is to minimise the experience - "It wasn't that bad", "He didn't really hurt me", "It only happened a couple of times", "Far worse things have happened to other people". Survivors minimise because to take on the whole experience, feelings and effects would be just too much to cope with. If you minimise you don't have to feel the whole of the pain.

Rationalising

Trying to rationalise the abuse, the reason behind the abuser doing what he is doing and the way in which he or she, the abuser, is behaving. For example "It's because he loves me", "He mustn't be well". Rationalising the abuse can make excuses for the abuser's behaviour, which may help keep the reality of the situation away from the survivor.

Hiding

Some survivors hide from the abuse and the feelings through throwing themselves into hard work, in school, and in later life at work, possibly overworking, putting everything into work so that no one will know - 'hiding' behind their work. Others hide behind bravado, drugs and alcohol in their attempts to stay away from the reality of the abuse.

Splitting / Detaching / Dissociating

When an experience has been so traumatic, the survivor can split off that experience so they don't have to see it as their own. This can range from viewing the child that this happened to as somebody else to actually appearing to have different personalities (multiple personality disorder). The survivor can express feeling for these 'others' - sadness, anger, hatred, guilt etc. - but can maintain the split so that the pain and feelings are kept at a distance.

Self Abuse

Survivors frequently have extremely low self-esteem and coping mechanisms that they sometimes use can be extremely abusive to themselves - e.g. drug and alcohol misuse and dependency are common when a survivor wants to forget and block out the pain. Sometimes survivors inflict pain on themselves in order to make visible, and to physically feel the pain they have inside. Self-injury, for the survivor, can often be positive and a means of expression. Self-injury is often looked badly upon and misinterpreted by 'professionals' as suicide attempts.

Self-Injury as
a Coping Mechanism

 Most people would deny that they ever self-injure, yet most people do in fact, at some point in their lives, do things deliberately to themselves that are harmful to their bodies and minds. Consider how people lie too long in the sun and burn themselves or smoke cigarettes and damage their health. Then there are the things that people do to themselves such as body piercing, tattoos and consuming alcohol. Not to mention punching walls through anger or frustration, overworking because of stress and binge eating when worried. All of these things are seen as normal by society because they are currently socially acceptable. Other forms of self-injury are not usually regarded as socially acceptable and are therefore seen to be a problem.

Self-injury can be very hard to understand, both for the person who does it and for those who provide support to them. The main thing to realise and accept about it, is that it is a way of coping with life. It is not madness or attention seeking. There are always very powerful reasons why a person hurts self and self-destructive though it may seem to be, self-injury is a way of surviving usually in the face of great emotional pain.

The reasons behind self-injury are complex and can vary tremendously from individual to individual. Self-injury almost always begins in response to painful and difficult experiences in a person's life. Sometimes these stem from childhood abuse and trauma, though it can also be part of the distress experienced in adulthood. Often there is no single cause that can be identified for self-injury, but it comes from a number of factors combining together in someone's life, which increase vulnerability and lead to a need to cope, or express self through self-injury.

Self-injury is often associated with abuse and many young survivors use it as a way of coping. One of the ways that self-injury helps someone cope is by giving them some way, however painful, of dealing with their feelings. Many people who self-injure feel unbearable distress, fear and tension. Hurting self can act as a kind of safety valve and can bring a sense of great relief, which can help the person cope better with life.

Self-injury can be about blaming self for something and turning the anger in on self. The person may take on all of the responsibility for events that he or she can't control, and so hurt self in order to punish self. The person may well believe that they deserve to be hurt.

Sometimes self-injury can feel like the only way that a person can release feelings. They may feel angry, sad, or anguished, and be unable to shout, cry, or speak to someone. Injuring self can, at the time, be the only means possible of expressing feelings.

Self-injury can be a way of avoiding dealing with feelings. It can be used as a means of numbing or distracting from the distress that is felt. In this way pain is used to distract self away from other emotions that the person is unable or unwilling to feel or deal with at that time. Pain can take someone away from more uncomfortable feelings.

Some people feel that if they did not release some of the emotional distress through self-injury, then they would actually commit suicide. In this case, self-injury is being used to stay alive.

Self-injury can be a way that people take control over an aspect of their lives. This may be the only thing in life that the person feels they have the power to control. Through self-injury she or he can have some control or power, even if it is only the power and control to inflict wounds on self.

Self-injury can be a way of trying to communicate with others. A person may need to make the pain they feel visible to self and to others. It can serve as a way of proving that he or she is hurting and in desperate need of care. There may be no other means of communication that the person can think of that can be used.

Self-injury might be used to express anger or frustration or as a protest about something. There may be no other means available of registering protest or releasing the feelings.

It may be used as a means of asking for support. The person may never have learned to ask other people for support; or comfort and support may have always been denied. Only through hurting self can some people then ask for support - ironically, support is then often denied because other people misunderstand what the person is doing.

Self-injury may not, to the outside world, seem like a logical thing to do, yet, for many people it serves the very practical purpose of helping them cope with life and stay alive. It has its own logic and serves a function for the person at the time. It is a normal response to stress, trauma, worry and distress.

Examples of Self-Injury

→ Cut with knives, razors, and glass.

→ Burn with fire, water, cigarettes, acid, bleach.

→ Swallow objects such as glass, batteries, pills.

→ Insert object into body orifices.

→ Pull out hair, pick at wounds.

→ Punch or hit self with objects.

→ Abuse drugs, alcohol and substances.

→ Binge eat, stop eating.

→ Deny medical treatment to self or go for unnecessary medical treatment.

→ Place self in dangerous situations.

→ Deprive self of sleep.

Myths about
Self-Injury

Self-injury is a failed suicide attempt.
It is a way of coping with life, not of dying. Injuries are seldom life threatening. A person may want to kill the feeling - not self. It can be a way of surviving through the many difficulties of life.

Someone who self-injures is a danger to others.
Self-injury is always directed at self not at others. Most people who use self-injury would never hurt someone else.

It is attention seeking and should be ignored.
Everyone needs attention. For some, self-injury is a desperate attempt to draw attention to the fact that something is wrong and they should have attention paid to their distress and its causes.

Many people who self injure hide their injuries from others.
It has far more to do with coping than with seeking attention.

The attention that self-injury frequently draws is usually very negative and further hurtful for the person. Seldom does it lead to helping a person feel better about self or relieving the distress that caused it in the first place.

Self-injury is done to manipulate others.
Like many other things, such as crying, talking, etc. this can be the case. However, by far the most important motivation is that it helps a person cope. It is about self - not about the effects of it on others.

Self-injury is an addiction or habit, which should be stopped.
A person hurts self because of distress, and it may be a coping mechanism, which has habitually been used, but it is not the behaviour, which is the problem so much as the pain and distress that gives rise to it. If someone is stopped without receiving help

for the underlying cause of it, they may develop a different coping strategy or hide what is being done.

People who self-injure enjoy the pain or do not feel it.

Nonsense! They may feel that they deserve pain or it may help them cope with a deeper emotional pain. Some people feel nothing at the time of injuring but later suffer immensely from the pain of the wounds or burns.

Self-injury is a sign of deep disturbance or madness.

This is not true. It is often a sign of great distress and of someone trying to cope with their life despite great pain. Many people who self injure manage to lead successful lives and have careers.

Safety and
Self-Injury

If the need to self-injure becomes so overwhelming that you believe the young person will go ahead - you can discuss safety with them. This is hard because it can seem like condoning self-harming behaviour, but it can save further distress.

Points to discuss with the young person

No matter what form the self-injury usually takes, try to ensure that the young person knows about the importance of making sure that anything used to cause harm is clean - this include the nails.

Talk to the young person about staying in control of what they are doing. Really letting go may cause greater damage than was wanted or is necessary. Suggest to them that they try not to self-injure when drunk or under the influence of substances as they may lose control of the situation.

Talk to the young person about cleaning the injury well. This is particularly important if they have not cleaned things beforehand. Depending on the nature of the injury, it is important to prevent infection. Good basic hygiene can help prevent this.

Suggest to the young person that they get information about basic first aid so that they know how to look after wounds. Provide basic information such as; for burns, run cold water over them until they cool, for cuts, clean using antiseptic wipes and cover with a clean dressing.

You can work with the young person on helping them make an emergency first aid kit for their own specific needs. This can be a positive piece of work to do with them, which can lead to an opening to discuss many other issues.

Talk to the young person about knowing when they might need medical attention. Many self-harmers do not want to seek medical attention but it is useful for them to know when they really ought to seek it. Medical attention should be sought if;

> Burns are large or deep.
> If a cut is deep and will not stop bleeding, apply pressure until it stops. If bleeding continues, then medical attention is needed.
> If an infection gets into the wound.
> If an overdose has been taken.
> If anything harmful has been inserted inside any body orifices and there is difficulty removing it.

Young people can be encouraged to go to the doctor, practice nurse, or the casualty department at the local hospital. They can take someone with them for support.

Let them know that:

> They have the same rights as other patients to be given pain relief.
> They have the same right as other patients to have treatment and to refuse to have a student observing or treating them.
> Treatment should not be dependent on them agreeing to psychiatric intervention.
> They should make it clear with the staff that what they did was not a suicide attempt.
> They can ask staff to explain clearly all treatment that they are to receive.

How the Young Women's

Centre Supports Young People

Young people can contact the Young Women's Centre in a number of ways.

- ➢ Drop in.
- ➢ Telephone us themselves.
- ➢ Someone telephone us on their behalf.
- ➢ They or someone else can write to us.
- ➢ They can e-mail us.
- ➢ Though one of our community groups.
- ➢ As a volunteer.

Regardless of the method of approach, our process of offering support is still the same and we try to gear the service to suit the individual needs of the young person. In the first instance, we meet with the young person, if possible, to tell them about the service we offer and to assess what the young person needs and wants. This first meeting is very informal and is always at the place and time that the young person chooses. The young person can have friends, family or anyone else present that they choose. In order to engage with the young person and begin the process of empowering, we meet them on their terms right from the beginning.

At the first meeting we provide as much information as possible about our service and any other services we know about. If the young person is too young to read our leaflets or is unable to fully understand, we provide the information to the carer or whoever has referred them and simplify our language to aid understanding. An example of this would be making sure that they understand what we mean by confidentiality. Rather than always using that rather big word, we will talk about who and what we will tell other people about, i.e. *"I will not tell your mum or dad or the police what you say to me." "I will tell your social worker if I know that your mum has hit you again, but I will talk to you first."*

At the first meeting, we tell young people about the different things on offer at the Centre to offer them as wide a choice as possible.

We offer:

➤ Regular appointments for face-to-face support.

➤ Telephone support through a free phone number.

➤ E-mail support.

➤ Daytime drop in.

➤ Volunteering opportunities with various accreditation courses.

➤ Advocacy.

➤ Befriending.

➤ Pregnancy testing.

➤ Accompaniment to other services.

➤ Group support.

➤ Activity groups.

For a young person who decides that they want to have regular one-to-one support, we match them to a support worker and they make an arrangement with their worker about how often and where they will meet. This is regularly reviewed and if the young person finds that they do not like or get on well with their worker, they can change to another worker. All the support workers are trained volunteers.

At the first meeting the young person is informed about our rules, the confidentiality policy and the complaints procedure. They are provided with an evaluation sheet and a stamped addressed envelope and encouraged to write down their views of the service and return the evaluation anonymously. **This process is repeated several times a year to make sure that we are providing the type of service that young people want.**

Centre Rules

Our rules are very simple and apply to everyone including staff, volunteers and service users. The rules apply in the Centre, during Centre activities or while on Centre business and they are designed to keep all involved safe. This includes workers not being placed in the situation of being a potential witness against a service user and thus having to breach confidentiality. For example the rule against stealing would cover a worker being with a young person who then gets caught shoplifting. The young person knows in advance that stealing is against the rules and what the consequences might end up being for them.

CENTRE RULES

> **No violence of any kind is allowed.** This includes name-calling, bullying, threats and all other forms of violence.

> **No drink or drugs.**

> **No stealing**.

> **No injuring self** on the premises or while with anyone from the Centre.

> Everyone must keep **confidential** about the identity of young people they meet at the Centre.

> **Respect** others and treat them as you yourself would wish to be treated.

> **Problems with others** in the Centre should be discussed with identified workers or a complaint put in to management to allow them to deal with it.

> Racism, sexism, homophobia and other prejudices are **not allowed** and have to be tackled with the help of the adults.

Confidentiality

We offer young people a very high degree of confidentiality but let them know that this can never be absolute. While we will maintain confidentiality to the extent that a young person can tell us about abuse they are still experiencing, there may be situations when we need to talk to someone else. Though we rarely breach a young person's confidentiality, a situation in which much younger children are involved would mean that the worker would be required to talk to the trained child protection workers. The young person would always be told about this and their permission sought.

There are very few situations in which we would ever breach the confidentiality of the young person outside of the agency. These situations, if they arose, would be discussed with the young person and the child protection workers and advice might also be sought from members of the advisory group before any action was taken. Our basic rule of thumb is that if we maintain confidentiality we must always be able to justify this action. Similarly, if we breach confidentiality we must also be prepared to justify this.

Support Work

The work we do with young survivors of abuse is varied and based on what they regard as their perceived needs. The young survivor dictates the pace and content of the support they receive. We see the young people who come to us as the experts in their own lives and provide support entirely on their terms. If the young person wishes to talk through what has happened to them, we will listen. If the young person prefers to listen to music, we will listen with them.

Our support workers take as long as the young person needs to build trust. We do not expect a young survivor to trust us at first; instead we build a relationship with them over a long period of time. Building the relationship can take the form of engaging in a range of social activities such as going bowling, swimming, to a café, outings, etc. In these we take our lead from the interests of the young person. When they are ready to talk to us about their problems, they can. The young person always sets the agenda and our job is to listen to them and believe them.

Support is open-ended in that the young person can keep coming to us as long as they wish. They can choose to end it at any time and can pick up on it again any time they choose.

Young people getting support from us can get involved in all levels of the organisation. They can come in and work as volunteers on such things as abuse prevention, peer education, befriending, administration and outreach. They can be elected onto the Management or Advisory group and can attend all meetings. The only area of activity that they cannot be involved in is direct support work.

We provide as much information to young people as they want on a variety of issues such as sexual health, housing, welfare benefits, drugs, alcohol, rights, legal issues etc. We also let young people know what other services exist which might be able to help them. We give them information about the police, health, education and social services, and inform them about other voluntary organisations. If the young person wishes to make contact with other agencies, we offer to help them do so, and accompany them if they wish this.

When working with young people we:

➢ Engage with the young person on their terms, in their time and at the place of their choice.

➢ Offer a high degree of confidentiality and explain what we mean by it.

➢ Take the time to build a relationship of trust.

➢ Communicate in whatever way the young person decides or needs i.e. through play, talk, drawing, etc.

➢ Work at the young person's own pace.

➢ Listen to and believe the young person.

➢ Encourage the young person to make decisions for themselves.

➢ Provide information to the young person.

➢ Work with the young person for as long as the young person wants us to.

Families

We will work with a family when a young person wants us to or when a young person is very young or has particular needs. Sometimes we find that it helps the young person more if we can provide support for a non-abusive parent. After all, it is the parent who knows their child best and often has to deal with the nightmares, difficult behaviour and flashbacks at home.

Often, we work with siblings who have not been abused themselves but who are struggling to come to terms with what happened to their brother or sister. We do always keep in mind though that our main client is the young person who has suffered abuse.

Crisis Work

Many young people approach us during a crisis. They can no longer cope with what is going on in their lives, and often can see no solution at all for themselves. With these young people we can often help by providing them with information, or assisting them in accessing another service which might be better equipped to help them than ourselves. Depending on what they perceive as the crisis we can often help them to take the steps they need to make changes in their own lives.

Besides having been abused, the most common crises for young people who come to us for help are; run away from home, fear of pregnancy, on-going abuse, homelessness, feeling suicidal, concerns about another child or a parent, and criminal activities. Depending on the crisis at the time we respond by encouraging the young person to talk, then offering as many options as we can. Most often this leads to contacting another agency such as police, social services or health services on behalf of the young person. We try very hard to make sure that the young person stays in control of the situation and makes the decisions about who to contact.

After the crisis is over, we encourage the young person to look at how the crisis arose and take steps to prevent it all happening again. Often underlying the repeated crises of young people is the fact that they are trying to cope with having been abused.

Working Together

The Young Women's Centre alone cannot provide everything that a young survivor needs. We are therefore very keen to assist the young person in building a network of support with other people and agencies. We work closely with social work, police, health, education and voluntary organisations if the young person wishes us to. We often effectively act as a bridge between the young person and other agencies, which they might not otherwise consider.

Working with other agencies is not always easy but it is worthwhile and often in the best interest of the young person. It is a good idea to get to know people in other agencies and what they do, before you need to contact them. It is also a good idea to have an agreed protocol between the agencies so that you know how they will respond and what their policies are, and vice versa.

When we work with other agencies, we mostly do so with the full agreement of the young person. We will attend case conferences, meetings and provide information when the young person wishes us to. On other occasions, when we are concerned about a young person, but do not have their consent, we might still speak with other agencies. We would do this by presenting hypothetical cases to agencies and asking how they would proceed or deal with the case. In this way, we can safely let young people know how other agencies will respond. This is often enough to encourage the young survivor to allow us to contact the agency officially on their behalf.

If the young person does not wish us to communicate with people in other agencies, we do not until the young person agrees. There are occasions though, particularly with much younger people, when we will, after consultation with our child protection workers, contact outside agencies without the permission of the young person. This would only happen in cases where we had very good reason to believe that the young person was in immediate danger.

While we find that it is better in the longer-term to share information with other agencies who are involved with the young person and the family, we also find that one of the most important things that we can offer a young survivor is our confidentiality. Once they have learned to trust us and know that we will not give out information against their wishes, they become much more open to the idea of agencies working together for them.

Dealing With

A Disclosure

For many young survivors speaking out about abuse is a major turning point in their lives. It is a moment of absolute vulnerability and the response of the person they disclose to is extremely important. Survivors may often test their listener with small pieces of information before full disclosure so that they can 'test the waters before jumping in'. The following are just a few guiding principles

Don't Panic

If a survivor speaks to you it is because they have chosen you and must trust you to some extent. Often people may feel they do not have the right skills to deal with it and rush to pass the survivor on to someone "who knows about these things". It is important to remember that if you keep a calm head and know the basics of how to listen, you will be able to handle it.

Listen

Many people are good listeners, but when some people feel under pressure they can talk too much. Survivors need space to speak and would find it off-putting if the listener starts on about "I know what you mean. Oh that must have been really terrible. Oh you poor thing, etc." There may well be moments of silence, the survivor may be working up to saying something important, so don't rush in or the chance will be lost. Obviously you need to respond to what is being said so that the survivor knows they are not talking to a brick wall, but the name of the game is giving plenty of space and making it possible for the survivor to speak.

Believe

Survivors are often disbelieved when they speak out. Many young survivors have already tried to tell someone and either not been able to be clear enough about what they were trying to say, or not been believed at all. This is common when the survivor speaks out in the family. The abuser, if named, may appear so respectable - aren't they always - and because of this, some listeners refuse to hear what the survivor is saying to them. Indeed, a lot of survivors expect not to be believed. After all, they have been living with the unbelievable for so many years! Remember that few people, if any, ever lie about a truly traumatic experience. The much more likely lie that young people tell is that nothing is happening to them at all, when it is.

Empower

The experience of child sexual abuse is a total loss of power and control. It is valuable to make suggestions and lay out options, but the final decision should be the survivor's. Even if you think that it is the wrong decision, respect her or his ability to make their own decisions. For example, most people agree that to speak out is a valuable and healing experience. But the survivor might not be ready to do that in a formal way, i.e. by contacting a survivors group. With younger survivors, many people want to rush and report the abuse to social work or police. The young person may not want this or be ready for it. Also, in doing this, things may get a lot worse for the survivor.

There is a real danger that the young person will retract his or her story if people rush to 'do something about it'. Obviously with a very young child this would not be the case and action would have to be taken, as the younger child would hardly be in a position to take action for themselves or have enough understanding of empowerment. The older the person though the more control they should be allowed

Don't try and make it better.

One of the most natural reactions in the world, when facing another human being in distress, is to try and make them feel better. A survivor disclosing abuse is not one of those situations when a nice cup of tea and a chat will do the business. Only the survivor has the power to make it better - by speaking about it and getting it out into the open. You as the supporter have a huge role to play, but it is secondary to that of the survivor - a message that many people should hear.

Support for the supporter.

Support for the supporter is very important and can be easily overlooked. Listening to a young survivor disclosing can be a painful experience in itself, but bear in mind that the pain is theirs, not yours to take away. Also remember that what they are telling you may have been, to them, a 'normal' way of life. However it can be the case that someone else speaking can stir up your own feelings to a degree that you need to share them with someone else. We highly recommend that you discuss the issue of support in this context. For example, how confidential will a disclosure be? What support is there for the supporter?

Recognise the strength it takes for someone to speak out about abuse. If you think about how hard it can be to talk to someone about a good sexual experience, imagine how difficult it may be for some people to talk about an unpleasant or traumatic one.

Remember no one asks to be abused or attacked and no one deserves anything like this to happen to them. It is never their fault.

Reassurance - you can reassure them that it was not their fault. They may have been threatened, or they may not have known what was going on. They may have been told over and over again that it was their fault. The blame **always** belongs with the abuser!

Summary of
YWC Support

Engage:

This is **best** done at the young person's pace, in the place of their choice and with whoever they choose to have present.

Communicate with the young person in language they understand, without patronising them and on their terms rather than your own.

Listen to them; believe what they say and reassure them that it is okay to talk and that everything they say will be confidential, in line with your policies.

Empower:

Offer information and options and encourage the young person to make the decisions about what they will do. The worker should then support them in the decisions they make. Recognise that the young survivor is the real expert on himself or herself and treat them accordingly.

Assess:

Be clear about what the presenting issues and possible underlying issues are with the young person. Identify what changes the young person wants to happen in their lives. Identify what types of intervention the young person wants or needs, and what you can realistically offer them, e.g. they may want or need, information, practical help, advocacy, befriending, support, counselling or a referral to another agency.

Plan:

With the young survivor, plan the work you will be doing with them. Involve them as fully as possible in this planning process. The planning should include short and longer-term goals and include regular reviews. It should also be flexible so that it can be changed by mutual consent.

Implement:

Make a date to start, agree the venue, set out any rules and boundaries and agree on what you can reasonably provide. Make sure that the young person fully understands any policies or procedures you may have, particularly regarding confidentiality about anything they talk about.

Evaluate:

Through **regular reviews** and evaluation of the results of these reviews you will be able to monitor what progress has been made. There is little point in continuing to carry out work if no progress is being made. By evaluating the work and making adjustments as necessary, the young person can get the best possible help available.

It is **useful** to record progress so that the young person can see for themselves the progress they have been making.

Support and
Empowering

Most of us support others in some way, yet few of us ever think clearly about the form of the support we are offering. When supporting, it is useful to be clear about what you are doing and why you are doing it, particularly in relation to young people. Young people's feelings and wishes are often overlooked in the adults' overpowering need to help them and this can result in the young person becoming further disempowered. Being aware of your own needs in a support situation is important, but be aware that the young person also has needs, and that these may differ from yours. Thoughts and feelings matter as well as actions. It is important to be clear as to your position and goals with yourself and your organisation, and at the same time be clear as to the position and goals of the young person.

There are many different skills involved in providing good, quality support to someone you are working with. The following is an outline of some of those skills.

VERBAL SKILLS INVOLVED

➢ **Language** - i.e. match your language to that of the person you are supporting. Do not talk over their heads or in language that the young person cannot understand.

➢ **Believing** - the importance of this cannot be emphasised enough. The young person is being expected to talk about personal feelings - they need you to believe them and not judge them.

➢ **Reassuring** - that it is okay to talk to you, that you will keep confidential, that they can stay in control.

➢ **Explaining** - e.g. anything you say to make sure it is properly understood, what the session is about, how long you have available, what you will do with any information provided, what your policies are.

➤ Paraphrasing - e.g. summarising what has been said to you, feeding back what the person has said for clarification.

➤ Questioning - ask if you don't understand something. Ask direct questions, e.g. how did you feel about that, how do you feel now, what happened then?

NON-VERBAL SKILLS

➤ **Body posture** - open and relaxed is good.

➤ **Body language** - watch your own and theirs. Sometimes a lot more can be picked up through this than through words, e.g. the person states they are not bothered by something they have said, but is fidgeting and uncomfortable looking.

➤ **Eye contact** - you need to use this but watch for the other person disengaging, looking away when struggling, finding difficulty because of embarrassment.

➤ **Facial expression** - stay interested in the young person you are supporting. Again, remember that the young person's expression may not match the words they are using.

➤ **Body movement** - Don't sit rigid but don't be shuffling about all over the place either. Watch closely the movement of the person you are supporting. i.e. someone beginning to curl up on the chair.

➤ **Quality of attention** - It's not enough to say you are interested and there to listen, you need to show it. By the same token, how attentive is the person you are supporting?

With all of the above, when you notice something, ask or say! Try not to jump down the person's throat though.

Some possible Support Approaches

The following is a starting point for thinking about the kind of support you might offer a young survivor of abuse, and its possible advantages and limitations. We would not propose any one form of support as being better than any other as young people and their needs differ. The kind of support you provide is for you and your organisation to decide and for the informed young person to choose.

The 'Rescue' Approach

This kind of support is about an adult stepping in and taking charge of the situation. This would usually happen and be seen to be quite appropriate in an emergency situation and can on occasions actually save the life of the young person. It draws on the reality of the supporter being in a better position to understand what is really going on for the young person and stepping in to deal with the situation. It is important with this approach, to acknowledge with the young person that the rescue took place, was really necessary and what the reasons for it were.

Possible problems with this approach can be;

→ The relationship between the helper and the young person may be damaged as the young person may disagree with the actions and necessity for the actions taken by the supporter.

→ The young person's sense of failure may be reinforced.

→ Dependency and powerlessness may result and repeated rescues as a form of support may become established.

→ The young person might do things and expect to be rescued at the wrong time. If the expected rescue doesn't then happen, the young person can end up in a worse situation.

→ The adult is making the judgement as to what is necessary. They may get it wrong.

The ' Freedom' Approach

This can allow the young person to learn through trial and error thereby allowing them freedom of choice in their lives. Trusting the young person to learn by themselves and from their own experience can be liberating for them and can increase their self-confidence.

Possible problems with this approach are;

→ This approach can often be seen as uncaring and irresponsible as the adult appears to be allowing the young person to take risks.

→ The young person may make a mistake and suffer a severe blow to self-confidence, or be hurt by the experience.

→ Adults usually believe in a 'right' or 'wrong' way to do something and may feel the need to intervene with the 'right way' rather than letting the young person learn their own way.

→ Leaving the acquisition of life skills to chance could be viewed as neglectful and inappropriate.

→ If the young person gets into difficulties, at what stage would intervention be appropriate?

The 'Keep a Grip On Them' Approach

In this approach, the supporter provides some external support in the form of keeping a close watch on the young person, albeit from a distance. This can provide a sense of security for the young person and allow the supporter to keep in touch with developments and share in the experience. It can prevent the young person from straying into more difficult areas and can provide direction and the possibility of immediate rescue should it be necessary.

Possible problems with this approach are;

→ This can restrict freedom to a high degree and lead to manipulation of the young person.

→ The supporter is in control of the situation most of the time - not the young person.

→ The supporter may like to feel needed and indispensable and be reluctant to let go the control.

→ The young person may become too dependent, or rebel against the external control.

The 'Look to the Horizon' Approach

This form of support encourages the young person to ignore the immediate difficult experiences and look ahead to the broader goals in life. In trying to identify possible goals for the young person and looking at possible ways of achieving these, the supporter attempts to focus the young person ahead and so ease their passage towards their goals. This may provide the young person with hope for the future and insight into their own experiences.

Possible problems with this approach are;

→ The goals the young person sets may be unrealistic and doomed to failure from the start.

→ The young person may have great difficulty focusing ahead if the situation they are currently in is very difficult.

→ The young person may believe there is no way forward and actually resent the optimism of the helper.

The 'Dive in beside Them' Approach

This involves the formation of a close relationship in which empathy and understanding of the young person's situation takes precedence. In this, the distance between supporter and young person is broken down and power and control is relinquished. The young person takes control over the process, the direction and the decisions and chooses the pace. Within this approach, the young person has the opportunity to take account of another within an equal working relationship. They can feel that they are not alone and have someone they trust to speak to.

Possible problems with this approach are;

→ This approach demands certain qualities in the supporter such as; openness, giving up the position of being an expert, loyalty, etc.

→ The young person sets the agenda and the supporter must accept this whether they agree or not.

→ The supporters may have to deal with their own feelings of wanting to intervene or take control of the situation.

→ The supporter may get bogged down with the young person's situation and be unable to continue to be supportive effectively.

→ The helper may lose the wider perspective of the situation.

The 'Provision of External Support' Approach

This form of support provides the young person with back up and cushioning in tackling a situation that may be new to them. This provides a safety net for the young person and allows them to gain confidence in their own abilities to face the experience.

Possible problems with this approach can be;

→ The supporter is making the judgment as to the form of support required.

→ The young person needs to be *'weaned off'* the external support as they gain in confidence or dependency will result.

→ The young person must learn to trust his or her own internal support system at some point in their lives.

→ Supporters must recognise that they can never fully prepare young people for what lies ahead, since each young person's experiences are unique to them.

The 'Give Instructions' Approach

Giving instructions on what to do and how to do it is a common form of support. The main requirement for this to work is that instructions be clearly given by the supporter, and fully understood and acted on correctly by the young person. This type of help can be of comfort to a young person, particularly in crisis situations. In this case, the supporter is taking hold of and managing the situation, so that an emergency is defused.

This approach works best only when the supporter allows the young person the space to make sense of their own experiences, and accepts that their experience may differ substantially from the supporter's perspective.

This form of support has great value on occasions, but as a regular response, its value is limited because;

→ The helper rather than the young person is the one who gets involved in understanding and exploring what is going on.

→ This approach is action centred and often cannot take account of the young person's thoughts or feelings.

→ The helper determines the action taken rather than the young person and this can lead to dependency.

→ Failure of the young person to follow the instructions correctly may result in confusion, distress and loss of confidence.

→ It does not allow the young person to learn or gain experience in dealing with other similar situations.

The 'Tell them how to Do It' Approach

In this form of support, the supporter tells or shows the young person how they themselves would deal with the situation. This information is not accompanied by any recommendation, and the young person is allowed to make decisions or take any action they think appropriate.

This approach works best as a two way process, which accommodates the reactions and contributions of the young person.

Several possible problems with this approach are;

→ The helper can assume that the information given has been understood- this may not in reality be the case.

→ The helper, drawing on their own experience, selects the information to give. This can lead to a gap in understanding or acceptance since the young person may not have enough personal experience to make sense of the information given.

→ To copy completely the actions of another is usually impossible and the young person may find it difficult to maintain a sense of individuality.

The 'Advocacy' Approach

This involves the helper in interceding on behalf of the young person particularly where the young person is having some difficulty dealing with adults. This approach acknowledges that young people are not listened to in the adult world and the approach of an adult on their behalf can smooth the path and help establish the rights of the young person.

Possible problems with this approach are;

→ By acting for them, the supporter may be reinforcing, rather than challenging the inequalities of young people.

→ The young person may come to believe that they are incapable of taking action for themselves.

→ The relationship between the young person and the supporter may be damaged if the young person feels helpless and frustrated.

The 'Throw A Lifebelt' Approach

This form of support involves the supporter in making the decision to act as rescuer when the young person is judged to be helpless and struggling. Throwing a lifebelt (of whatever sort) helps by removing the young person from the situation and guarantees their immediate safety.

Possible problems with this approach are;

→ Sometimes the supporters are responding to their own sense of helplessness. This may not be the feeling of the young person at all. The young person on being rescued may say that although they were struggling they were managing.

→ The young person, while being rescued at the time, may have to return to the difficult situation and still be ill equipped to deal with it.

→ The supporter may feel *'good'* about the rescue while the self-esteem of the young person may be damaged.

→ The young person may feel powerless and demoralised by the experience.

No matter what form of support you and your organisation chose to offer, it is vital that young people know in advance what you are offering them. This does more than anything to empower young people in that they can make informed choices in advance of speaking to you.

General Guidelines
for Support

1. **Be familiar** with the different forms of support.

2. **Be aware** of the form of support, or combinations of support you are using and their pros and cons.

3. **Ensure** that the young person is aware of the form of support you are offering and that the young person agrees with it.

4. **Be aware of** your own needs and expectations and the needs and expectations of the young person.

5. **Take account of thoughts and feelings,** both for the young person and for yourself.

6. **Stay human.**

7. **Clarify** where you stand on the issues of power and authority.

8. **Remember** your overall purpose or goal in helping young people.

9. **Remember** the young person's overall purpose and goals in seeking your help.

10. **Think** of the consequences for the young person and yourself before you act.

11. **Don't panic!**

12. **Try** to be aware at all times of the perspective of the young person. Think yourselves into their shoes but remember whose life it is.

13. If you **cannot** help the young person effectively, refer them to **someone who can**.

In Support,

Young People Need

To be allowed and encouraged to express their feelings of sadness, shame, guilt, anger, etc

➢ To know that their reactions to the trauma are normal reactions.

➢ To be helped to realise that they are not in any way responsible for what happened to them.

➢ To be told they have rights: to feelings, to be loved and cared for, to be protected from harm.

➢ To know the abuser/s are always to blame for what happened.

➢ To know they are not alone.

➢ To recognise fully what has happened to them.

➢ To accept they are not "damaged" for life.

➢ Reassurance that it is okay to speak and they will be listened to and heard.

➢ Allowed access to any information they need or want about rights, sexuality, resources, etc.

➢ To be allowed and encouraged to seek additional support for themselves as and when they need and want it.

REMEMBER

➤ **You are not the cavalry.**
   You are there to support young
   people in whatever way you can, not to
   live their lives for them or rescue them.

➤ Young people need to be taken seriously
   and believed when they speak to you.

➤ You need to allow time for trust to build and not to
   promise what you can't deliver.

➤ You need to let young people know that you believe
   them, and reassure them that it is right to speak about it.
   Body language and tone of voice are very important in
   this.

➤ You need to let young people know that you care, it's
   okay to say you feel bad about what they've gone
   through and that you admire their courage in speaking
   out.

➤ Stay aware of how patronising adults can be.

➤ Young people can tell in a flat emotionless way. Do not
   assume by this that they have no feelings or problems.
   This may just be a way of coping.

➤ Young people can sometimes be aggressive or difficult -
   no wonder!

➤ Remember that young people may have no reason to
   trust you at first. You have to earn their trust.

- Remember to listen carefully and give your undivided attention - no chatting between adults.

- The younger the person, the harder it is for them to think that there is any alternative to abuse. Younger people have little sense of themselves as individuals with rights.

- Change may sometimes be perceived by young people as the end of the world.

- Some young people tend to blame themselves for everything.

- You will have to be prepared to give lots of time and commitment and sometimes give this at short notice.

- Get lots of support for yourself.

Tips for Supporting Young Abuse Survivors

- **Be clear about the time you have available.** Don't initiate talking when you know that you are going to have to rush away to a meeting in a few minutes.

- **Find a private, safe space free from interruptions.** Try to ensure that the space you have chosen is warm and friendly but without too many distractions such as a telephone that might ring periodically. Put a *'do not disturb'* sign on the door and tell people not to knock or come in while you are talking to the young person.

- **Try not to rush things.** The young survivor will need time to think as well as talk and may become overwhelmed with flashbacks and panic from time to time. Talking is seldom easy.

➤ **Don't panic at what you are hearing.** The young person before you has survived and has now found the courage to begin to talk. Overreactions on your part may delay or stop the survivor talking. It is easy to overreact when you hear a younger survivor speak but it is best to take the time to think clearly before you take any action. Though you may struggle to hear what the young person is saying, and it may be the most awful thing you have ever heard in your life, try not to get too emotional in front of the young survivor. They may think that they have upset you by talking and could withdraw from talking about the abuse.

➤ **Be aware** that you may not have the whole picture. Most young survivors give a little bit of information first rather than it all at once. There may be much more to things than you have been told already.

➤ **Don't** assume the abuse has ended even if the survivor is talking as though it has. This is often the last thing to come out.

➤ **Do not use** patronising language with a young person. Though young people are used to this, they rarely like it.

➤ Treat the survivor with **respect.** They deserve your respect and in sharing with you are taking a big chance on you.

➤ **Believe** what the survivor is saying to you. Survivors expect not to be believed, yet belief is one of the most important things that a survivor needs. It costs you nothing to listen and believe in the first instance.

You can gently challenge any apparent inconsistencies in the story as trust in you grows. Young people often tell in a garbled manner when they first begin to talk and often are talking about a range of things that happened over a period of time. The story seldom comes out in a chronological and coherent manner. The story you hear at first may sound very confusing but if you give the survivor enough time, it usually begins to make sense after a while.

➢ **Tell** the survivor that he or she was not to blame. Most survivors feel to blame for what has happened to them and it is important that supporters let them know that the abuse was not their fault. Keep telling the survivor this.

➢ **Reassure** the survivor that it is okay to talk about things and that you will believe what you are told. Constant reassurance is usually necessary, as the survivor may believe that it is disloyal or wrong to tell. The many fears that are around for the survivor will need to be addressed in time, but a constant reassurance that you will listen and it is okay to tell you can go a long way to beginning to address some fears.

➢ **It is important** to acknowledge what she or he is saying and feeling. This lets a survivor know that you have been listening and accept what feelings are around. Let the survivor know that whatever they feel is normal and valid. Crying is okay, even for males. Being angry is allowed and normal.

➢ **Be honest** with the survivor! Do not make false promises that you may find out later can't be kept. The best example of this is telling a survivor that you will be able to get the abuser to stop. This may not actually end up being the case so it's better not to say it.

➢ **Be very clear** about your roles and responsibilities as a worker. You may not be able to do all you would like to for the survivor as it may not be seen as part of your remit. Also, if there is likely to be a police investigation into an allegation of abuse, it may not be in the best interests of the young survivor to be questioned by you.

➢ **Try** not to 'rescue' the survivor. Much as we often feel that we could help by jumping into the situation on behalf of the young person, this is not always the best course of action to take. Rescue by an adult is not always possible or even desirable. More often the need to rescue comes from the feelings of the adult supporter. Stop and think, talk to a colleague and take advice before you jump in to affect a rescue.

➢ **Be clear** and up front about where you stand on issues of confidentiality **before** the survivor speaks.

➢ **Do not** blame the survivor or imply blame with statements such as, 'why didn't you tell?' or 'why did you do that then?' This type of second-hand blaming often comes from the frustrated adult who knows that they could have helped out earlier if they had only known. It is better to take things from where they are now and praise the survivor for talking to you now.

➢ **Find out** what resources and services are available for young people with specific problems in your area. There may be other agencies that can provide help. Often, after a disclosure, agencies such as police, education, health and social services are brought in to help, but there may be other agencies that can offer a different type of help. For example, there are many voluntary agencies such as rape crisis, drugs and alcohol projects, befriending agencies for young people, etc. Voluntary agencies can often provide longer-term support round specific issues.

➢ The young survivor may have very **mixed feelings** about the abuse, the abuser or the disclosure. She or he needs to be allowed to express these feelings and work through things at his or her own pace. The survivor cannot work to other people's timetable or agenda.

➢ It is important to **empower** young survivors to speak and make informed decisions, as far as possible, for themselves. It is important for survivors to retain some control over their lives.

➢ **Keep the survivor informed** about anything that has a bearing on his or her life. As far as possible, they should be allowed access to written records, attend all meetings pertinent to them and have a say. This is their life!

➤ If the young survivor has other support either from an agency or an individual, **encourage this support** to continue. This is especially the case where a young person is removed from home and taken into care. They should be able to hold onto the important and non-abusive people in their lives. If the young survivor has no other support, help her or him to find some. You can't do it all.

➤ **Know your child protection policy,** and what you must do within your agency, preferably before you ever get a disclosure from a young person.

Above all stay calm.

Common
Problems

While abuse is happening young people find many ingenious ways of coping with it and surviving. They have no choice in this. The longer the abuse goes on the more adept they become at finding a way to accommodate it and live. The young people learn to adapt to their lives and appear as normal to the outside world. Often they cope better with the abuse while it is happening than when it has ended.

This is especially the case for young people who have never known anything different. Sometimes when abuse ends the young person finds it very difficult to adapt to a life free from abuse. While living with abuse, they were simply surviving from day to day, but when it ends they then frequently have to deal with the thoughts and feelings about what happened to them.

Flashbacks

Most survivors of abuse experience sudden intrusive and disturbing thoughts and memories, which they find very distressing and difficult to deal with. This tends not to happen until the abuse comes to an end. Many people think that with the ending of abuse all will then be well with the survivor. This is rarely the case.

Flashbacks can come as small bits of memory, a whole complete memory, intense feelings and emotions or a mixture of memories all jumbled together. Though on occasions survivors can work out a trigger for what caused the flashback to come when it did, more often it seems to happen out of the blue.

These memories are often so intense and distressing that they completely overwhelm the survivor. Frequently survivors believe that the traumatic experience is actually happening to them. They can feel the pain, smell the smells and experience the whole event over again as though it were happening for the first time. Some survivors experience flashbacks as pictures, sensations or like a video recording playing over and over again in their minds. Many feel absolutely helpless when it is happening and feel that they can do nothing to stop it or control it.

Helping During Flashbacks

There is a great deal that a supporter can do to help a young survivor deal with the experience of having flashbacks. First you need to know that that is what's happening. If a young person isn't able to tell you, you can often guess what is happening. If the young person suddenly seems to switch off from you and appears to become very preoccupied and inward, there must be a reason. Also if the young survivor seems frightened, appears to be regressing or seems to suddenly be in pain, it is possible that they are having a flashback. Only the survivor really knows so it is important to try very gently to find out.

While in flashback it is very difficult for survivors to say what is going on for them, but as they move out of it you can let them know what you observed and try to get them to talk about what was going on for them. Let them know that they do not need to talk in detail about it until they want to or feel able to, but you can get them to talk generally about what just happened and where their thoughts went.

A young survivor can become extremely distressed by flashbacks and it is a good idea to discuss with them (while they are not experiencing it) strategies that can be used to get back in control. You can agree with the young survivor things that you can try to help them stay grounded in the here and now and things that they can try when you are not there.

Things you can offer to do - get consent from the young person first:

➢ Keep talking to them to try and keep them present.

➢ Get them to notice other sound such as birds singing outside, a clock ticking in the room, etc. Often sound is the last sense to go in a flashback and many survivors are reassured by knowing that you are still there and they are still in the room with you.

➢ Hold your hand out and tell them to reach out to you. If they do, suggest that they can pull themselves away from the memory and suggest they do so by pulling on your hand.

➢ Hold their hand to offer a physical contact that helps them realise that someone is with them who will not hurt them.

➢ Hug them to offer safe physical contact and reassurance.

Things the young survivor can do:

➢ Identify an object such as a teddy; a piece of jewellery or even a stone picked up on the beach as their grounding tool. When a flashback begins, they hold onto the grounding tool so they know they are in the here and now.

➢ Get hold of a good memory and every time a bad memory comes, they try to replace it with the good memory.

➢ Find a good strong piece of music and play it or sing it to themselves every time a flashback starts.

Survivors need reassurance that the flashbacks are a normal response to trauma. They need to know they are not mad. Many people rush to take young survivors to the doctor because of flashbacks and though this may sometimes help them, pills are seldom the long-term solution.

Ultimately, when the young survivor is ready, talking about the painful memories can eventually sort them in the mind and lay them to rest. Some survivors talk, some write or draw or find other ways to deal with the intrusive memories and most survivors over time stop having the flashbacks.

Panic Attacks
Another problem for young survivors can be panic attacks. These are very distressing and often just appear out of the blue. Sometimes they happen during or after flashbacks. Sometimes they happen for no apparent reason. A panic attack is very frightening. The heart races and flutters, sweat breaks out, breathing becomes fast and more difficult as there are often intense feelings of terror. Frequently the feelings are so intense that the young person believes they are about to die.

Because the attacks are so dreadful, the young person may try to avoid the place it happened in. Sometimes the panic attacks happen when the young person goes out of the house. This can lead to the young person not going to places they normally would or even stopping going out. There are ways of helping the young person deal with these attacks and the sooner they are tackled, the less chance of them developing into a major problem.

Things that can help:

> Being with the young person to reassure them that they are going to be okay.

> Reminding the young person to breathe properly. Sometimes breathing into a paper bag can help if the young person starts to hyperventilate.

> Suggesting they go to the difficult places with a friend.

> Suggesting they try talking or singing to themselves when it begins. Even counting backwards from one hundred or saying a rhyme or the alphabet has been known to help.

> Reminding the young survivor that they have survived the abuse and can survive and face up to the fears.

Nightmares

Many survivors experience terrible nightmares, which can cause major sleep disturbances and exhaustion. If the young person is not talking about the trauma and bottling things up, it often surfaces through nightmares. Sometimes when a survivor begins to talk the nightmares get worse. Some survivors become afraid to  go to bed and go to sleep, as they are so terrorised by the nightmares they are experiencing. Often the only thing the survivor remembers are the feelings that the nightmare generated in them and they have no memory of the nightmare to link them to. Other times the nightmare is so vivid that the memory of it lasts for days at a time. Again the survivor can be reassured that it is normal to experience nightmares and they will stop.

Things that can help:

> It can often help to talk, write or draw pictures about the nightmare.

> If the parents or carers are caring people they can encourage the young person to talk to them as soon as possible about the nightmare and reassure them that they are now safe.

> If wakened by the nightmare, doing things such as; getting up, having a drink, taking a bath and playing music before trying to go back to sleep can sometimes prevent the nightmare from recurring.

> Doing relaxing things before bedtime such as having a bath (if this isn't scary for the survivor), playing soft music, cuddling into someone safe.

> Changing the bedtimes can sometimes make a difference. If the young person isn't at school or has no reason to get up early, they could sleep in the morning or the afternoon for a while.

Obsessive Behaviour

Some young survivors become quite obsessive for a while after the end of abuse. They may for example refuse to walk on cracks in the street, be particular about the order they dress in, wash repeatedly, etc. This too is quite normal behaviour following a trauma. If a young person has been abused they were rendered powerless and had no control over their lives at all. Even in the aftermath of abuse they may have had no control over the proceedings, including no say in what happened or where they might live.

Often these young people are simply taking control of the things they feel that they can control in their lives. They may go too far in this for a while but often it is a way of them beginning to regain control over their own lives. Many people worry about the beginnings of obsessive behaviour in a young person and occasionally professional help will be needed. Mostly though the young survivor does come through this phase by themselves or with gentle help from a parent or supporter.

Things that can help are:

> Not avoiding talking about the behaviour or just ignoring it in the hope it will go away.

> Tell the young person what you are noticing about the behaviour and offer to talk about it with them.

> Ask them if they notice what they are doing and if they know what it's about.

> Letting the young survivor know that it is a normal response and they are not nuts. Many will think they are and be worried about it.

> As with all responses and problems, be prepared to suggest professional help as part of the options available to the survivor.

Support for
Workers

Surviving Working with Abuse

If you are someone who works constantly with abuse, you need to learn to take good care of yourself. Working with abuse, especially the abuse of children and young people, can begin to impact on you and affect both your work and your home life if you are not careful. Workers can lose insight, become over-involved and spend every waking moment thinking about the survivors they are working with. Frontline workers can be affected by what they hear and see, particularly if their caseloads are too large and they have little support within their agency. Unfortunately this is all too common in some agencies.

One of the things you need to safeguard yourself from is burnout. Often workers fail to realise that they are beginning to reach the stage of burning out and that everything is getting on top of them. Many continue to take on more and more work until they are exhausted. These workers can begin to display similar symptoms to trauma survivors and if they continue to work on at the same pace, may eventually become very ill.

The other thing that can happen when working with survivors is that unresolved personal issues of abuse may be triggered. Workers can be survivors too, and may feel that they have dealt with their own abuse or managed to bury it. Suddenly they find that the memories and all the associated feelings have come back into their minds at a time when they least expected it. The worker is then in the position of trying to support a survivor while their own issues have suddenly surfaced. Workers can become very overwhelmed by this and need support themselves to deal with their own issues.

Dealing constantly with abuse can also lead to secondary trauma for workers and cause them to suffer from a kind of post-traumatic stress. They experience the destruction of their world-view and begin to lose hope. Sometimes they become depressed and even suicidal and can end up needing medical help to recover.

Most of this is preventable. Workers need to be able to keep a strong self-awareness about how they are and what they are feeling. They need to be able to empathise with the survivor but not fall into the feelings trap. They need to know the difference between their own feelings about hearing about the abuse and the feelings of the young survivor.

Workers also need to have a good system of support and supervision so that they can off-load and explore issues and feelings that have arisen for them. Good working relationships in a supportive environment can help a lot, but time set aside with a good supervisor is vital to being able to continue working with young survivors of abuse. Workers must be able to talk with someone in confidence and be able to talk about how the work is affecting them in a way that is open, honest and supportive.

It is important that workers in this field are able to maintain balance in their lives. They need to be able to switch off and relax. They need to be able to say no to doing more work than they feel capable of. Everyone has a limit to the amount of stressful work that they can realistically take on and despite the many young people out there in need of support, no one person can do it all. When workers reach capacity, they and their managers must learn that a refusal to take on just one more case can make a difference to the worker's ability to continue working effectively.

Each agency and each worker within it should recognise that if they need to pull back or stop taking on any more work, others will step into the breach and pick it up. It is also better to provide good quality sustainable support to one person rather than a haphazard and ineffective service to hundreds.

We need to recognise in the first place that we are in need of support or that support might be a positive thing before we can do anything about it. The agency needs to recognise that supporting its workers leads to less stress, less illness, better work and more effective use of the available resources. Workers need to recognise that they are not infallible, or weak, that they might benefit from support and that it is not a waste of valuable time or a threat.

Internal

Support

People should, where possible, seek the support of another worker. This could be an informal lunchtime chat. We all need to be aware that feelings are important, everyone has feelings whether they
show them or not and anyone can be struggling in some way. It might be a good idea to acknowledge this and offer support where needed on a one to one basis. Time needs to be set aside and allowed for this. We each need to take some responsibility for seeking support for ourselves. No matter who the person is, or what position they hold in the agency, everyone needs support sometimes. The work place needs to be a safe enough place to ask for, and expect to get, quality support for one another.

A climate of support can very easily be established in any work setting. All this involves is getting into the habit of asking colleagues how they are, especially after they have dealt with a difficult situation. No one should ever be going from one intense situation to another throughout the day without ever having the space to either say how they are feeling or let off steam. While it is the responsibility of a worker to seek support, it is also the responsibility of colleagues to check in with the worker when they know a difficult situation is being dealt with. Asking for support is in reality a strength, not a sign of weakness. Giving support is good for all and leads to a far stronger and more focussed team.

Group Support

During work or team meetings some time could be spent focussing on the need to rebuild as a team. You could occasionally work together through some group exercises such as team building, stress management, etc. A time during meetings could be used to check out how people are feeling about their work, and, if necessary, set a time for individual workers to get support. Positive feedback within the work team can go a long way to changing negative experiences and attitudes.

Even when someone has made a mistake, rather than the team focussing on the things that were done wrong, a positive outcome can be reached. Each mistake we make is a learning experience, and, though it can be easy to blame an individual, that is never constructive in the longer term. Accept and admit that none of us are infallible, learn from the things that go wrong, and stand together as a team. A strong team is a supportive team.

External Support

For some individuals, for various reasons, there is a need to recognise that the only way they will be able to get adequate support is from outwith the organisation. This will obviously need to be agreed by the organisation beforehand. Individuals who are in need of external support could be allowed to contact support workers, in confidence elsewhere. There are organisations and individuals who can offer confidential support to workers from any agency. There are professional counsellors who can be accessed (though there might be a cost to the organisation). There are therapists, voluntary and statutory bodies who might be approached for external support.

Structured One to One Support

The biggest difficulty in setting this up is often the reluctance of the agency and the workers to see this as necessary or important. It may take a little bit of encouragement to get people to try this out in the first place. If this can be worked out though, once people try it out, they usually find the process beneficial.

A minimum of an hour could be set aside every month for this. Two hours is even better. The place used for support should be carefully thought about. It is better to be away from telephones, including mobiles. Best to be in a comfortable area with tea and coffee and also smoking facilities for any smokers. Quiet, calm and undisturbed is the order of the day in this. The best way to ensure the individual support works is to set the dates in advance for this. Structure can be negotiated between the agency and individuals in advance, and can be changed and adapted to suit individuals.

Suggested Structure for One-to One Support

Begin by putting the person at their ease; (the cup of tea and small talk bit). This shouldn't take too long if you already know the person, and they welcome the support session. Where someone isn't sure or is fairly new to you, it might take a little bit longer at first.

Agree an agenda and try to facilitate keeping to it.

Check out how the person is feeling about their work in general. Find out if there are specific problems with colleagues, workload, time management, etc. Don't spend too long at this unless there are big problems. This stuff should be dealt with in supervision sessions. You can suggest, if there are problems, that the person speak with their supervisor or colleagues. Don't get into problem solving.

Move on to asking the worker how they are feeling. You will probably get the reply "I think" coming in to the equation. Listen then ask again. Try to keep the workers focussed on their own feelings. Ask specifically how he/she is feeling about particular areas of work. The worker will probably start to talk about the person they are working with. Again, listen till you get the gist of it, then push things back to try and get them to explore how they personally feel. This bit can be quite hard. The supporter will need to stay very focussed. Gentle reminders can be thrown in about the session being for them to explore their own feelings. Encourage the worker to be honest at least with self. Let the worker know that it's okay to be a bit 'off' i.e. feeling pissed off at survivors and their needs.

Depending on what is thrown up by the worker, the last bit of the session can be used to look at ways of safely dealing with feelings, setting up a personal support network, reassuring that it's okay to have these feelings, and winding down.

REMEMBER

➤ **Listening is vital**. You listen and they talk.

➤ **Be gentle.**

➤ Go at the pace of the worker you are supporting, but don't let them wriggle out of things. Sometimes, the thing the worker most needs to talk about is hard, and they will take the easy option and divert away from it.

➤ **Be reassuring** and honest with the worker. Especially in regard to what you mean by confidentiality.

➤ There's nothing wrong with being direct if you want to know something. **Ask!** At the end of the day the worker can always decline to answer if they really don't want to tell you something.

➤ **Stay focused**. When people begin to bring feelings into things they sometimes go off at the most incredible tangents. You can gently bring them back if you stay focussed.

Other
Related
Issues

Trauma and

Child Sexual Abuse:

A child or young person who has suffered sexual abuse has suffered physically, but they also have a lot of mental suffering and distress to cope with both at the time, and in the aftermath of the abuse.

Powerlessness. They suffer the loss of the world, as they knew it. Up until the intrusion of the abuse they had only experienced the world in one way. For many of them this was a relatively safe world. Abuse rips that safe world away from them. Often they feel trapped and completely helpless in the face of the catastrophe of abuse. If the abuser is known to them, as most often is the case, they may lose love or become very confused by what love really is. They also suffer from an extreme loss of control, and of boundaries. All of this is very confusing to young people, and the feelings of powerlessness can be overwhelming.

Fear. A young survivor of abuse often feels extreme terror sometimes mixed with tense excitement. Other strong feelings such as a fear of being killed, fear of disapproval or fear of loss can also confuse and overwhelm them.

Lack of Understanding. Children often cannot make any sense of what is happening to them. They frequently suffer from a total incomprehension and bewilderment as to what is going on and being done to them. They often have so many questions that they are unable to ask anyone, with no answers available anywhere.

Betrayal. Sexual abuse of a child is such a complete betrayal that it is nearly impossible for a young person to comprehend. They find out that there is no safety in a place they have always felt safe. They discover that trusted adults tell lies. They suffer a complete loss of trust and often end up believing that there is no protection anywhere.

Intrusion. Sexual abuse is a catastrophic, forced, unnatural, violation of body and space. It is invasive in nature, not just of the body, but also of spirit and identity.

The trauma of sexual abuse leads to a disruption of sense of self and development. It is a mental health matter that often has severe consequences for the child. It can lead to a distortion of self and can flood the mind with strong negative feelings. It is not only a physical trauma; it is a mind trauma also. It can often interfere with good mental health and is usually not forgotten even into adulthood.

Mental Health

Growing up can be difficult. Young people are under stress to be liked, do well in school, get along with their families, and make important life decisions. Most of these pressures are unavoidable, and worrying about them is natural. Sometimes though the pressures and stresses of life lead on to poor mental health, and occasionally mental health problems develop.

Mental health problems are real, painful, and can become very severe. They can lead to school failure, loss of friends, or family conflict. Young people who have been abused are vulnerable and abuse can seriously affect the good mental health of a young person. Even very young children can suffer from mental health problems, including depression. More than 25% of young people have problems in life, they are vulnerable, not coping, fearful of change, have difficulties with relationships, have been abused, suffered losses.

Young people face many obstacles in life. For all of them growing up is not easy. They face many difficulties such as, development, peer pressures, demand for jobs, loss of childhood dependency, changing and growing, coping with changes in body and mind, control, frustration, fears, power, understanding.

There are two categories of young people with problems; those who turn inwards and those who turn out. They may respond by withdrawing, getting involved in crime, self harm, becoming suicidal, destructive behaviour.

Mental Health Problems

Depression: Depression is an expected and fairly normal response to significant loss or chronic stress. Abused young people experience a series of significant losses and stressful events as a result of their abuse. To experience problems functioning in virtually every area of life coupled with coping with the aftermath of disclosure or continuing to live with the abuse, probably warrants some level of depression. Therefore, it is probably accurate to say that, to one degree or another, most abused young people experience depression.

Although it is difficult to assess the difference between depression, which accompanies abuse and depression as a separate clinical disorder, there are key characteristics that assist in the differentiation. Abused young people talk about feeling depressed; however, depression may not be the primary emotion noted during the recovery process. Rather, young people experience guilt and self-blame which centre on their feelings of the abuse and the abuser. For example, young people talk about feeling ashamed of the sexual acts, how their bodies responded by feeling pleasure, their inability to say no, and their not even knowing that it was wrong.

Loss of interest in activities and social isolation are also characteristics of depressed young people. Abused young people frequently experience depression as they struggle with particular memories or feelings. Coming to terms with abuse means dealing with grief, anger, rage and many other feelings as well as coping with the feelings of the parent or carer. Often the young person feels to blame about the hurt caused by the disclosure of abuse.

Major Depression: Young people most at risk of experiencing depression as a primary problem are young people who have a history of trauma, chronic stress, and significant loss. Family members and significant others frequently trace the young person's sadness and deterioration in functioning directly to the loss or trauma. They may express concern, however, that the young person declines to talk about it or admit to any feelings about it whatsoever. If ignored, unresolved grief and trauma will become issues, which contribute to depression. This is why trauma should be addressed.

While suffering bouts of depression in an abused young person is fairly normal and will often disappear through time, there is the danger that it can lead on to more serious depression. It is better never to take the risk with a young person's mental health. Encourage the young person to talk to a doctor early on in any depression. Most depression responds positively to anti-depressant medication, although the drug selected may take up to three or four weeks to have an effect.

 Pills alone will not be effective in depression and emotional and practical support is vital. There needs to also be an attempt to better understand the psychological factors that caused the depression to occur at this time. For example, a young person may have low self-esteem, an attitude that increases vulnerability to depression. He or she may need to learn to express hostile and assertive feelings and may not fully understand the difference between reasoned, controlled expression of feelings and an angry outburst. Thus, many depressed young people are individuals who tend to trap their angry feelings inside themselves, producing a self-imposed passivity.

People with depression may gain substantial help from someone who simply listens attentively to their concerns; others need help thinking through the solutions to external problems that may contribute to their depression.

A depressed young person is more likely to get into various forms of trouble through displays of challenging behaviour. However, it's not always clear whether he or she is in trouble because of being depressed, or whether the depression comes from being in trouble. But once symptoms are numerous, severe, or long lasting, it doesn't matter *"which came first"*; evaluation and treatment by a qualified professional are needed.

Manic depression is another form of depressive illness. A person with manic depression has mood swings that fluctuate between extreme highs and lows. This is another illness for which treatment is necessary and often effective. Manic-depressive illness usually starts in adult life, before the age of 35. Although rare in young children, it does occur in teenagers. This illness can affect anyone. However, if one or both parents have manic-depressive illness, the chances are greater that their children will develop the disorder. Manic-depressive illness may begin either with manic or depressive symptoms.

Schizophrenia is a medical illness that causes strange thinking, strange feelings and unusual behaviour. It is an uncommon psychiatric illness in children and is hard to recognize in its early phases. The behaviour of children and young people with schizophrenia may differ from that of adults with this illness.

The behaviour of children with schizophrenia may change slowly over time. For example, children who used to enjoy relationships with others may start to become more shy or withdrawn, and seem to be in their own world. Sometimes youngsters will begin talking about strange fears and ideas. They may start to cling to parents or say things, which do not make much sense. The child's teachers may first notice these early problems.

Possibly the saddest fact about depression is that much of this suffering is unnecessary. Most people with a depressive illness do not seek treatment, though the majority, even those with the severest problems, can be helped.

Some of the signs that may point to a mental health problem are listed below.

→ Feeling really sad and hopeless without good reason and the feelings don't go away.

→ Feeling very angry most of the time.

→ Cries a lot or overreacts to things.

→ Feeling worthless or guilty.

→ Feeling anxious or worried more than other young people.

→ Grieving for a long time after a loss or death.

→ Being extremely fearful, with more unexplained fears than most kids.

→ Constantly concerned about physical problems or appearance.

→ Feeling frightened that his or her mind is controlled or is out of control.

There are other telltale signs pointing to a crisis in a young person's life. Look for big changes in the way he or she deals with normal, everyday experiences, e.g.

→ Does much worse in school.

→ Loses interest in things usually enjoyed.

→ Has unexplained changes in sleeping or eating habits.

→ Avoids friends or family and wants to be alone all the time.

→ Daydreams too much and can't get things done.

→ Feels life is too hard to handle or talks about suicide.

→ Hears voices that cannot be explained.

→ Has poor concentration; can't make decisions.

→ Is unable to sit still or focus attention.

→ Worries about being harmed, hurting others, or about doing something *"bad"*.

→ Needs to wash, clean things, or perform certain routines dozens of times a day.

→ Has thoughts that race almost too fast to follow.

→ Complains of persistent nightmares.

Of course, there are other behaviours that necessitate intervention as soon as possible. Be on immediate guard if a young person:

→ Uses alcohol or drugs.

→ Eats large amounts of food and then forces vomiting, abuses laxatives, or take enemas to avoid weight gain.

→ Continues to diet or, exercise obsessively although already bone-thin.

→ Often hurts other people.

→ Destroys property, or breaks the law.

→ Does things that can be life threatening.

Suicide and
Young People

All suicidal ideas that young people express are serious and must be treated as such. Suicidal feelings may give way rapidly to suicide plans and actions and are best not brushed aside. Even quite young people can feel suicidal.

It is often hard for adults to believe that a young person is feeling suicidal. They often find it unnerving and threatening and can find it easier not to believe that the young person is serious in intent.

It is best to try and find out more about the young person's feelings. Talking about suicidal feelings will not encourage young people to act on them but ignoring them might.

Listening to, accepting and taking feelings seriously is the best way to build trust. Trust makes it more likely that they will accept your help.

Get information about other services in your area and give it to the young person. Encourage the young person to seek help.

You can help by:

➤ Listening not lecturing.
➤ Helping them to deal with stress and emotional pain.
➤ Introducing them to problem solving techniques.
➤ Increasing self-esteem by giving plenty of praise and encouragement.
➤ Helping enable independence of the young person.
➤ Staying involved and supportive of them.
➤ Helping them to find an investment into the future.
➤ Being aware that they need support before a crisis, hopefully to help prevent one, during a crisis and after a crisis.
➤ Remembering there is a stigma about mental health problems and try not to label young people.

Child Abuse and

Domestic Violence

Domestic violence is a very common form of abuse, generally directed at women and their children by partners and ex-partners. Such abuse can be very extreme, and consists of emotional, physical and/or sexual abuse sustained over a long period of time. People frequently try to avoid getting involved and believe that if the children are not actually experiencing the abuse then it is doing them no harm. This is not the case.

Children often know what's going on no matter how hard a parent tries to hide things from them. What they don't know they often imagine from what they hear. They often hear arguing, shouting and fighting. This is abusive in itself and can cause tremendous fear and many problems for the children. There is a growing bank of evidence that witnessing abuse can have severe adverse affects on the children.

Children living with domestic violence frequently see the effects of the abuse on their mothers. They may see cuts and bruises and see their mother very frightened. More often they directly witness the attacks and many children are themselves physically attacked by the abusers. Many of these children live with extreme terror on a daily basis.

There have been several studies carried out regarding possible links between child sexual abuse and domestic violence and there certainly appears to be some growing evidence of links between them. This is hardly surprising as domestic violence is very much about the abuser using power and control to dominate, suppress, and abuse another person. Sexual abuse is also about abuse of power and control. Any person capable of this with an adult is only a small step away from doing the same with a child.

Domestic violence within the home can also hide child abuse that might be happening. Most children who are being sexually abused live with threats and are too afraid to tell about the abuse.

If their mother is in a violent relationship it can increase the child's fear of the abuser - *"He beats mum up - he may do worse to me if I don't allow him to do what he wants"*.

If their mothers are being abused it shows them to be in a powerless situation - the children are in an even more powerless situation. They may believe that their mothers cannot do anything to get away or to help them.

Children may not say anything about the sexual abuse, due to the fact they know their mother is being abused. They may not want to add to any upset or pain and may see a disclosure as doing that.

The abuser may repeatedly tell children, who live in situations of violence in the home, that their mother is stupid, and deserves it. They may be encouraged or forced to participate in ridiculing her. This can create barriers between the mother and her children. The children may even blame the mother for not protecting them.

Child sexual abuse depends on secrecy - living with domestic violence can enhance this secrecy. Mothers whose children are acting differently may just put their behaviour down to the violence that is happening in the home - while the real reason for their behaviour can be due to sexual abuse.

Women who are abused by violent partners may feel they are protecting the children by staying and putting up with it. She may believe that if he is hitting her, then he will leave the children alone. The abuser may have threatened to keep the children if she dares to leave him. The woman's fear of this can be very great and also realistic. Many abusive partners fight through the courts for access to, and custody of, the children. This gives them immense power over the woman. Some women understandably crack under the strain of living with the violence, and are then labelled as having mental health problems. This makes it all the more likely that he will get the children, and be able to use them to control her.

If the partnership breaks down entirely and the woman gets away, he usually still has access to the children. This is an ideal situation for an abuser to continue sexual abuse of children.

Women who have discovered such abuse and have tried to report it are regarded as being malicious and vindictive towards their former partner. Many women and children are simply not believed.

Children may be affected by violence within the home by:

→ Witnessing or overhearing abuse of their mother.

→ Intervening in the violence to try and protect their mother thus risking violence to themselves.

→ Intervening by trying to seek help, phoning police, relative, neighbour, etc.

→ Being totally controlled.

→ Being encouraged or forced to humiliate their mother.

→ Being terrorised by the abuser through what they witness, threats and abuse.

→ No money being available for new clothes, shoes or even food.

→ Domestic violence creating an ideal opportunity for the abuser to physically, emotionally or sexually abuse the child.

The fact cannot be ignored that domestic violence always has an adverse affect on other family members, especially the children. This is the fault of the abuser, not the abused.

Myths and Facts about
Domestic Violence.

Domestic Violence will not affect the children.

Children may witness or hear domestic violence taking place within the home - this is abusive to the child emotionally and mentally. If a child tries to protect their mother from the violence, even by disclosing it is happening, they may well risk physical abuse.

They want it or enjoy it - if they didn't they would leave.

There are many reasons why a woman may not leave an abusive relationship. These may include; she has nowhere to go, she has no money of her own, she can't leave the children, she could be too frightened to get away, it'll get worse if she tries to escape, she blames herself, or her partner will kill her.

They ask for it, deserve it or provoke it by nagging or refusing sex.

This is just an excuse for violence. Refusing sex is any woman's right. No one can provoke anyone to carry out abuse on another person; the abuser makes that choice, not the woman. No one deserves to be abused mentally, physically, emotionally or sexually.

They tell lies and exaggerate - it was only a fight.

Generally the perpetrators of domestic violence come out with statements like this which minimise the abuse to try and make it sound 'not as bad as it really is.' The real lie that happens is in protecting the abuser, or being too afraid of the abuser, so covering it up by saying that the latest bruise was just an accident.

If they had fought back they could have prevented it.

Why should a woman ever be in the position of having to fight back? It is surely meant to be a partnership. Men are generally physically stronger than women, so it is often difficult or impossible for women to fight back. If women did try and fight back they could end up with much more serious injuries. He could prevent it by just not doing it in the first place.

It only happens in certain types of families.

This again is incorrect. It doesn't matter what type of background you are from, no one ever deserves to be abused. Domestic violence happens in all types of families. This is again trying to shift the blame from where it really lies - with the abuser.

Alcohol causes domestic violence.

This is not a cause. This is another excuse. Domestic violence occurs, whether or not the violent partner is drunk. Drink sometimes releases the inhibitions of the violent partner and 'allows' for even more violent behaviour. Many people manage to consume alcohol and not become violent towards others. On top of that, the abuser rarely assaults others; he picks only on his partner.

Abused women tend to be violent towards their children.

This is simply not true. A lot of women believe that because they are receiving the violence then they are protecting their children from the same treatment and in general can be very protective of their children. Many women go to great extremes and take many risks to try and protect their children from the abuser. Women living with domestic violence are no more likely than anyone else in the population to be violent towards their children. It is much more likely that the abuser will be violent to the children than the abused woman.

Women in violent relationships where the children are being sexually abused must know or be able to tell what is going on.

Child sexual abuse relies on secrecy, manipulation and distancing a child from its mother. Children can be distanced from their mother by never being allowed to be alone with their mother, ridiculing the mother, showing the children pornography, etc.

The violence may make the children see their mother as ineffective and weak. The children may be led to believe their mother knows about the abuse and is condoning it. Some children will not say anything due to the fact they know about the domestic violence and don't want to upset their mother further.

Women living with domestic violence are no more likely to know about sexual abuse of their children than any other parent. Abusers are very skilled at ensuring the child does not disclose.

Young people can experience Domestic Violence in very much the same way as adult women as the following extract from our training pack shows.

Scenario:

- ✗ She gets beaten, nipped, punched, choked, kicked and slapped.
- ✗ She gets put down and called names.
- ✗ She gets spat on, insulted and humiliated.
- ✗ She gets locked in, locked out, set up and controlled.
- ✗ She is not allowed to go out without his permission.
- ✗ She is not allowed to look at or talk to another male.
- ✗ She is not allowed to wear what she wants.
- ✗ She gets accused of having affairs.
- ✗ She gets blamed for everything he does to her.
- ✗ She gets raped and sexually assaulted.
- ✗ She has no money of her own.
- ✗ She is very afraid of him.
- ✗ She is afraid that if she tells anyone or tries to leave he will abuse a child.
- ✗ She can never please him, no matter what she does.
- ✗ She does not want him prosecuted or sent to jail.
- ✗ She loves him.
- ✗ She needs his love.
- ✗ She wants him to stop hurting her.

- ✗ He often says he's sorry and that he loves her.
- ✗ He is sometimes very loving and affectionate to her.
- ✗ He has sex with her whenever he chooses - no matter what she thinks, feels or wants.
- ✗ He calls her stupid, ugly, cunt, bastard, slut and whore - never by her own name.
- ✗ He is unpredictable in mood and action.
- ✗ He controls the home and all the money.
- ✗ He threatens to kill her.

The Woman:

She is 13 years old! *He is her father!*

She needs to get out. Her most basic needs are for shelter, food and warmth. What are her choices?

Shelter?

Women's Aid?	**No.**	She is too young.
Safe House?	**No.**	She is too young.
Homeless Unit?	**No.**	She is too young.
Salvation Army Hostel	**No.**	She is too young.
Cyrenians?	**No.**	She is too young.
Friends?	**No.**	They are too young.

Money?

Social security?	**No.**	She is too young.
A job?	**No.**	She is too young.

Or she could try social work and/or the police....

Social work will help her **if she can tell** about her father. The police will prosecute if there is enough evidence. Her father will be contacted and told what she says. She will be sent back home to her father if she does not (or cannot) tell about the abuse. It is not enough for her to just say she will not stay at home.

Or she can run away and live rough on the streets.....

She could beg....

She could steal.....

She could sell her body.....

Or she could find a man to look after her.......

Young people who find themselves in the situation as outlined above are extremely powerless to take any action and make changes in their own lives.

Helping Young People who live with Violence at Home

Awareness: Perhaps the most important thing is to be aware that domestic abuse nearly always affects young people who are living with it. Often alongside domestic abuse of a parent, children are emotionally, physically, or sexually abused. Most young people for a variety of reason are reluctant to disclose this at the time. At least if supporters are aware of the potential for direct abuse of young people in this situation, they may be more able to pick up on any clues that this might be an issue.

Talking: Young people need to be able to talk freely about what is going on for them and their feelings about it. Even very young children can find ways to express themselves if they are encouraged. Younger people can draw, paint, use play equipment or music to express how they are feeling. Though there may be nothing practical which can be done to help young people, talking about things can be a way of preventing them bottling up their feelings. They can be encouraged to let out their feelings about the violence in a positive and healthy way that can be less damaging to them longer-term.

Before they talk though it is important to be clear about what degree of confidentiality you can offer them. You may, for example, be in the position of working with the family and feel the need to share some things that the young person says. This could damage your relationship with the young person if you have not been clear beforehand.

Support: Practical and emotional support could be provided to young people to help them cope with the violence. Practical support can take the form of finding resources, helping with forms, etc. Emotional support often involves being there for them, listening, believing, and, sometimes, safe human contact.

Options: Young people seldom know what options exist for them. With very young people there are generally fewer options, but as they get older this changes. Options might include living somewhere else, phoning the police or a relative for help, finding other agencies, which can help, etc.

Reporting: Young people need to know that they have the right to report domestic violence if they want to. They also should be informed if you are required to report anything to anyone. There may be occasions when you, or your agency, feel that you ought to take some action, it would be preferable if you do this with the consent of the young person. Obviously, with much younger people, adults need to think about the welfare of the child ahead of anything else. Sometimes this may even mean going over the head of the non-abusive parent. When people live with abuse, they may be too afraid to act appropriately. Once away from the abuse they may see things more clearly. Where possible though, reporting abuse to anyone official ought to take account of people's wishes.

Access: Even when young people leave situations of domestic violence, abuse may continue. Adults make the decisions about this and although older young people's views are taken into account, generally, if the adults insist on access to their children, and there has been no disclosure from the young person, they get it. Abusers with access to the young people may continue to abuse them, try to turn them against the non-abusive parent, usually the mother, try to get information such as addresses out of them and generally continue their controlling behaviour. Though access can be supervised, it seldom is. Sometimes, young people who are living away from the abusers home feel safe enough to make a disclosure. In this case, if the non-abusive parent then reports it, they are often seen as vindictive and just not believed.

Prostitution

There are many reasons for young people becoming involved in prostitution and though many people judge these young people and consider them to be making an active choice, this is not always the case. In any case of child prostitution the child is being abused by the adult who pays for her or his services. The child cannot be held responsible for the actions of adults and should be provided with support rather than condemned by the system.

Many adults who work in prostitution have reported being abused as children. Often this leads to low self-esteem, lack of ability to say no to others, disregard for their own feelings and the belief that they are only there to be used sexually. Some come to the conclusion that what was taken from them in the past can now be paid for.

Choosing

Some young people choose to sell sex as a way of getting the luxuries they want. They are either unaware of the danger they place themselves in or simply do not care. There are many adults who take full advantage of this and are prepared to give money and gifts in return for using the young person sexually. While it might seem that these young people are choosing what they are doing, many of them are far too young and inexperienced to make such decisions. These young people ought to be protected from the many adults who are seeking to prey on them.

Being Trapped

Some young people get into relationships with older people who are seeking young vulnerable people to abuse. They fall in love, believe that the person loves them in return and through a process of careful grooming at the hands of the abuser, end up trapped in a situation of being prostituted. The abuser is at first loving towards them but in time changes and begins to manipulate the young person into doing what they want. Often the young person becomes so desperate to please the abuser that they will do anything for them. Because the demands of the abuser over time become more and more extreme and the punishment for not giving in to the demands also becomes more extreme, the young person becomes too afraid to protest.

Family Set-Up

Some abusers, even within family settings, introduce the young people they are abusing to prostitution. As these young people are already conditioned to accept being used by adults for sexual purposes, they are much more accepting of their situation than others. Most people are horrified to discover that this actually happens, but it is only an extension of what the young people already experience at home. In some cases it begins with the abuser sharing the young person with friends and other family and moves on to selling the young people for sex. Some young people are forced to go out on the street and seek adults who will pay for their sexual favours. Often these young people cannot return home until they have raised a specified amount of cash.

In some more highly organised abuse situations involving groups of abusers, the young people are used to find other like-minded abusers who are then drawn into the activities of the group.

Sometimes the young people are used to find adults who are open to sexual approaches from children. The young person can then take the adult into a situation where other adults can get photographic evidence or videos, which can then be used to blackmail them.

Often young people who become, for whatever reason, involved in prostitution are a very short step away from being used in pornography. The two can run hand-in-hand and the young person can be used in both. Pornography is very big business and there  is a huge hungry market out there, which is always seeking more and younger victims. The use of the Internet has greatly expanded this market and the young people are readily preyed upon to satisfy the lust and greed of adults. In all of this, the young person is the innocent party, no matter what they are forced to do, or how willing they appear to be.

Prostitution- you can help young people by:

> Not judging them.

> Listening to them and believing them.

> Taking the time to build a relationship with them.

> Suggesting that they use the protection of condoms to prevent pregnancy and sexually transmitted diseases.

> Helping them access other services and getting them condoms if necessary.

> Exploring options with them.

> Letting them know that they can take control of their own lives.

> Letting them know about normal relationships.

> Helping them to see that the people who pay them for sex are exploiting them.

> Helping them to see that they are not to blame for what is going on in their lives.

> Finding ways to get the abusers away from them without damaging your relationship with the young person.

> Offering practical help and options such as looking at their accommodation and money needs.

Pornography

Pornography can be used in the abuse of children and adults in a variety of ways.

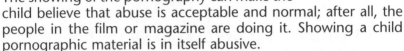

Showing the child pornography as a way of 'softening up' the child before the abuse. This may then lead on to touching and fondling, in time leading to further more extreme abuse. The showing of the pornography can make the child believe that abuse is acceptable and normal; after all, the people in the film or magazine are doing it. Showing a child pornographic material is in itself abusive.

The child may be shown pornographic material as a form of degradation towards their mother, building barriers between the child and mother, which in turn can lead to prevention of disclosure. Again it's making the child believe that this is normal, acceptable and can also lead on to further abuse.

Using the children for pornography. Some people believe that if child pornography were freely available it would prevent child abuse - this is a complete myth! The children used in the pornography would have to be abused in the first place. They may be forced into sexual activities with other children, adults or animals, while being photographed or filmed.

Child prostitution and pornography - using children to engage in sexual activities at a price, filming the child in various situations including being sexually abused for other abusers to buy and watch at leisure.

There is often a progression of events leading up to a child being used in pornography.

→   Showing the child pornographic material to get them accustomed to it.

→   Bribing the child with gifts, sweets and money.

→   Using threats to force the child to be more involved and not tell.

→ Getting the child used to being touched and stroked while watching or reading pornographic material with them.

→ Engaging the child in 'gentle' sexual acts at first.

→ Accustoming the child to the use of cameras and videos, at first recording fairly innocent scenes but gradually moving towards sexual acts and extremes of abuse.

→ Reproducing and circulating the pornographic materials amongst other abusers.

Children are powerless in all of this. They rely on adults to provide them with love and security. When an adult chooses to abuse this position of trust and power, the child often becomes completely powerless to stop the abuse. Adult survivors who have been used in child pornography may have fears over the pornographic videos and pictures, which may still be in circulation.

Pornography - Facts and Myths

Legalising or liberalising pornography would lead to a reduction in the number of sex crimes committed.
The idea of making pornography freely available would be in the hope that it would reduce sex crimes. It doesn't. In Denmark "serious" sexual crimes e.g. rape, assault and battery connected with sadism have risen by more than 5% since pornography has been legalised.

If pornography were freely available, people would soon lose interest in it.
If this were true then sales of pornography would be dropping. This is not the case. Pornography is a massive growth industry.

Pornography is really only for the tourists.
Pornography is not a seasonal thing. It is available all year round and is purchased all year round. As said earlier, pornography is a massive growth industry. If it were only for "tourists" then this would not be the case.

Children can be adequately protected from pornography.

Pornography is sold everywhere and is freely available in newsagents. It is now unavoidable. Even children can buy pornography in the shape of some newspapers. There is also no way of stopping an adult purchasing pornography to give or show to a child.

There is nothing abusive about pornography.

*In pornography women are portrayed as **willing** participants to acts of rape and sexual violence. This is not always the case. Evidence from many survivors of sexual violence tells of a forced involvement in pornography, child abuse and rape. Any child involved with pornography is being abused, whether or not they 'consent' to it.*

Women who participate in pornography do so of their own free will and some of them enjoy it.

Many rapes shown in pornography are actual rapes. Homeless people and runaways can fall prey to the offer of some "easy" money. Some women do it due to having no choice; either that or their family will go hungry. In America it is estimated that approximately 75% of women involved in pornography have been abused at some point in their lives.

Because some lonely men have access to pornography, it saves women who they may otherwise assault.

Even if this were true it would not explain the fact that in Denmark "serious" sexual crimes increased when pornography was legalised.

Providing child pornography would prevent the abuse of children.

This would not be the case. To start with children would have to be involved in the making of the pornography, which in itself would be abusive. Which children do we sacrifice to test out this theory?

Pornography - you can help by:

➢ Campaigning against it.

➢ Building links with the young person so that they can tell you what is happening.

➢ Not judging, listening to them and believing them.

➢ Helping them access other services and agencies.

➢ Exploring options with them.

➢ Letting them know that they can take control of their own lives.

➢ Helping them to see that they are being abused if they haven't worked this out yet.

➢ Helping them to see that they are not to blame for what is going on in their lives.

➢ Finding ways to get the abusers caught without damaging your relationship with the young person.

➢ Offering practical help and options such as looking at their needs.

➢ Using all the other support skills as outlined elsewhere.

Parents and Carers

Protecting
your Child

Most of us want to protect our children from harm and have them grow up as easily and painlessly as possible.

Unfortunately, as we all know, there are many dangers throughout childhood and it is impossible, and, indeed, unhealthy to be with your child twenty-four hours a day, seven days a week.

Children are inexperienced and vulnerable in the world and as parents, we do our best to teach and equip our children with the awareness and skills they need to survive to adulthood. So we teach them not to play with fire, never to hang out of windows, how to cross the road safely and be aware of the danger of strangers. The big area we often neglect, however, is sexual abuse. This is often because we do not think about it, don't believe it could happen to our child, or don't know how to address it with our children.

Unfortunately, if we do not make our children aware of the danger of such abuse, it can make them even more vulnerable. In a recent survey in Dundee, 1 in 7 children said that they had been sexually abused. Also given that most children are not abused by strangers, but are abused by trusted adults, it is vital that we teach them how to stay safe and how to get help.

Obviously, we do not want our children to be afraid of every adult they know or meet. Nor do we want them having nightmares about all the terrible things that can happen to them. But we do want them to be aware of potential dangers and of staying safe. **So how do we, as parents and carers, achieve this?**

Sensible

Safety Steps

Though not all abuse can be prevented and there is no guaranteed right way to safeguard children, there are some very sensible things that parents and carers can do to help reduce the risks to the children.

➤ Teach your child that they have rights.

➤ Talk to your children from an early age and encourage them to always feel that they can talk either to you, or to another adult.

➤ Tell them about other adults who can help them. You can mention other relatives, friends, teachers or anyone else you can think of.

➤ Teach your child about feelings. Give them the language they need to talk openly about feelings.

➤ Teach your children to listen to their own feelings and encourage them to share them with you and others.

➤ Tell them that they are important in their own right and that no one has the right to hurt or frighten them

➤ Teach them that their body belongs to them, and them alone and that no one has the right to touch them in a way that they don't like or want. Respect this yourself, even when they don't want hugs and kisses from you.

➤ Tell them that they have a right to fight, yell, scream, say 'no' to any adult, or run away to a safe place if they can.

➤ Tell them that it is not their fault if someone frightens or hurts them and it is still okay to tell you.

Sensible Safety Steps continued:

➤ Tell them that no adult (or young person) has a right to hurt them or do anything sexual to them.

➤ Teach them which areas of their bodies are private to them i.e. genitals.

➤ Talk to your children about how to tell if anyone ever hurts or frightens them.

➤ Tell them if no one listens to them at first, to keep on telling until someone does listen.

➤ Listen to your child. Learn from them.

Suspicions
of Abuse

As parents and carers, you know your children better than anyone else. This means that you are your child's first line of defence in the fight against abuse. Often parents can be the first to suspect that the child has a problem or worries. It can be that your child's behaviour changes in some way, (e.g. bed wetting, playing truant, being aggressive or withdrawn, etc.) or you may notice sleep or eating problems. While it may be that there is a perfectly reasonable explanation for your child's behaviour, it is always best to try and find out what is actually going on for your child.

It is not always easy to get to the bottom of any problems your child may be experiencing, and sometimes when you do, it is easy to trivialise them or dismiss them as unimportant. It is important that you always try to listen to your child. Something that is trivial to you might be a major worry for your child. Also, if you get into the habit of listening your child will be more able to tell you if something more serious happens to them.

There is no one right way to go about finding out what is bothering your child. Sometimes, parents worry so much about how to go about it that they become incapable of doing anything for fear of getting it wrong. You can try broaching the subject openly and casually with your child. An opening such as, "I notice something is worrying you just now, would you like to talk about it?" can work wonders in giving your child permission to talk. Make sure that you will not be distracted and that you have the time to listen. If your child doesn't wish to confide in you, suggest other adults that they might try talking to, tell them that they have a right to get help to sort out worries and that often talking to an adult can help.

If the direct approach doesn't work, try asking someone whom you know the child likes, to try and talk to the child on your behalf (a family member, close adult friend, teacher or doctor might do.)

If you get no joy here and you are still worried, talk to your child's friends and ask them if they know what is wrong. Tell them you can probably help your child and that it is okay to talk about problems.

If you suspect that your child has been, or is being abused it is important to get help to deal with it. Don't dismiss it. It may be that your suspicions turn out not to be true, but it is important to make sure that your child is safe. You can talk to a close friend about your suspicions to check out what they think and may have noticed. After all, two heads do often think much better than one, and your friend may be able to think of something you haven't. There are voluntary agencies such as The Young Women's Centre, Victim Support, Rape Crisis, Samaritans, etc. who you can speak to in confidence about your concerns. Voluntary agencies can often help you get more information on what action statutory agencies will take, if any, and can help you contact them if you wish.

You can also contact the social work department or the police yourself and they will investigate any suspicions you may have. Most areas have specialised joint social work and police child protection workers who might be able to help.

Parents/Carers and Abuse

Most parents would agree that every child deserves to be loved, cared for and kept safe from harm. The majority of parents and carers do try to provide a safe and loving home for their child and try to protect them from harm. Despite parents and carers best efforts though, sometimes a child does get hurt and parents can feel concerned or worried about their child. It can be particularly traumatic for parents to discover that their child has been hurt in a sexual way, especially if the abuser is a close relative or trusted friend. There can be many unresolved feelings and difficulties in coming to terms with the abuse.

If you discover that your child has been raped or sexually abused, you may feel a range of conflicting emotions that change over time. Everyone has a different response to a traumatic event but some of the most common feelings are listed here.

Feelings of Parents/Carers

If your child has been abused you will have many feelings of your own to deal with in addition to looking after your child's needs. Feelings of being a failure, out of control, anger, rage, helpless, despair, unable to see any future, disempowered, depressed, unable to support the child, self blaming, guilt, sorrow, powerless, vengeful, can't cope, suicidal, emotional, alone.

→ You may feel completely numb and unable to feel anything at all.

→ You may feel you have let your child down in some way or failed to protect him/her from harm.

→ You may feel angry towards yourself, your child, your partner, the abuser or no one in particular.

→ You may feel unable to cope with anything at all. Everyday tasks might feel too difficult to manage for a while.

→ You may feel depressed or even suicidal and feel that there is no point in going on.

→ You may feel guilty or to blame for what has happened to your child.

→ You may feel helpless or despairing.

→ You may feel totally isolated and alone.

→ You may feel that you need someone to talk to.

Feelings

of the Child/Young Person

Some of the most common feelings for young survivors of abuse are: guilt, anger, betrayal, confused, not believed, no trust, dirty, frustrated, desperate, no self worth, self blame, embarrassed, unloved, isolated, no one to talk to, worried, feeling different, alone, scared of people, powerless, suicidal, can't concentrate, no future, upset, mood swings, feel responsible for the feelings of the family, out of control, struggling, worried about pregnancy, shut down, withdrawn, unimportant, hurt, fearful, grief, lost childhood, bad, self destructive, will never be okay again, etc. Feelings can and do change over time and depend on the individual and the particular situation the young person is in.

Guilt and self-blame - Often the child feels to blame for what has happened and for the distress caused to the family when the abuse is disclosed or found out. Often the abuser has said that it is all the child's fault.

Betrayed and distrustful - Young people should have been protected from harm by adults and if they are abused by an adult or someone known to them they are, in effect, betrayed and can lose all trust in adults.

Not believed - it is regrettably common for young people not to be believed when they first try to tell. Often they try to tell someone and no one listens to them or understands what they are trying to say. Sometimes they do not tell for fear of not being believed.

Worried and desperate - It is sometimes difficult for young people to understand what has happened to them and they may become worried about pregnancy, HIV, people knowing, police and courts, causing family break-up, upsetting parents, etc.

Angry - Young people may feel very angry that they were not protected, even when there was no way the parents could have known. They may feel angry with themselves for not fighting or not stopping it, or they may feel angry with everyone.

Alone - When children are abused, they often feel totally alone in the world. They may feel that no one can love them and that they are the only person that this has ever happened to.

Embarrassed - Adults do not talk about sex or about abuse and young people recognise that it is a taboo subject. This means that it can be extremely embarrassing for the young person to share intimate and traumatic details with parents.

Scared - Young people may feel very scared especially if they see their parents' anger. Often they believe that the parent is angry with them for telling.

Sad and withdrawn - Sometimes, young people become overwhelmed with feelings of sadness and feel lost and bewildered by the events.

Disgusted and dirty - They can feel that they are dirty and feel total disgust at themselves, their bodies and about what happened to them.

Helping Your Child Recover

Young people can recover from the trauma of sexual abuse but their recovery often depends on how other people, particularly parents or carers, respond to their needs and feelings.
You can help by;

➤ Believing your child and helping them to make their own informed decisions.

➤ Listening when your child needs to talk and give time and attention when it is needed.

➤ Not Blaming! Regardless of the circumstance, it was not your child's fault that he or she was abused. No young person can ever be to blame for the abuse they experience. The abuser is always the one who is to blame.

➤ Reassuring that they were right to tell about the abuse even if it has taken a long time to tell you. Constant reassurance can help your child to continue to talk about it.

➤ Reminding your child that, if you are angry or upset, it is not at him or her or because of telling, but because of the abuser and the abuse that has been suffered.

➤ Praising your child's courage in speaking out and trusting their ability to survive.

➤ Informing your child about what is happening or is going to happen. This is especially important if you are going to take action as a result of finding out about the abuse.

➤ Giving your love. Telling your child that you still love them. Hugging and comforting your child can be comforting for you also but it is important not to force it if your child doesn't want to be touched by anyone just now, even you.

➤ Getting help and support for your child and yourself, if needed. Finding out about any other help or support that is available and telling your child about it or helping her/him access it.

Possible Problems for Families Of Sexually Abused Children

The family may **not be believed** by the outside world. This can be especially true if the child has named a person who is well respected as a 'pillar of society'. People often take sides with some believing the named abuser and disbelieving the child, and others taking the side of the child. Just remember that children seldom lie about things like this even though it is often difficult to prove.

The family can become very **isolated**, with people avoiding them, speaking about them, and generally not wanting to know. It is often as though the family is blamed for exposing others to a dreadful reality that people do not want to accept, or believe can exist, in their community. Your real friends will stick by you but they may find it difficult to know how to support you. Tell them what you want and need from them.

The family can become **split** if a family member is the named abuser. Sometimes members of the family choose to believe the abuser and side with him/her even in cases where the abuser is convicted. When the abuser is not convicted, it becomes even harder to accept what the child has disclosed.

There can be **divided loyalties** within the family. This often arises where members of the family love both the abuser and the abused and it can be difficult to know what to do or say for the best. Try to remember though that the child who has been hurt is the victim of a serious crime and much as you care for the abuser, that person should be made to face up to the consequences of his or her actions.

There can be great **losses** i.e. financial, home, etc. If the abuser owns the home you live in, or you are financially dependent on that person, you and your family can lose a great deal. The safety of the children must however be the most important issue here. Housing departments, women's aid, rape crisis and the social work department may be able to help you sort things out.

There can be the loss of the future (hopes, expectations). It can be devastating to find that all your hopes for the future have been wiped out. You may need to grieve about this and get support for yourself and your family but in time you can rebuild your life.

The family can feel very **exposed** and can be targeted by their community. This is especially the case if the abuser has been or is in the home or has abused other children in the community. In this case, the whole family, especially the children, can suffer the vengeance of others.

A Few Don'ts for Parents

➢ Don't restrict your child's play or activities - they may see this as punishment for what has happened, even though you may just be trying to protect your child from further abuse. Instead encourage your child to be aware of potential danger and to talk to you if they have fears or worries.

➢ If the child is clingy for a few days after the abuse has been disclosed don't be afraid to let him/her just hold onto you. They may need a lot of reassurance over a long period of time.

➢ Don't ask probing questions about the details of the abuse. If the abuse is reported to the police or the social work department, your child will have to go into detail with them. Some children can't give parents intimate details, or they may feel pressured into talking about something they don't want to talk about. They may try and forget the whole thing, hoping that you will too.

➢ Try not to say, *"Why didn't you say No?"* or, *"Didn't you realise it was wrong"* or *"Why didn't you tell someone sooner?"* This type of remark can increase your child's feelings of guilt or self blame.

➢ Don't make any promises about not telling anyone or of what will happen to the offender. You may have to tell the police and it is possible that there will not be enough evidence to convict the abuser. It is important for the child to able to trust what you say therefore, it is better to say that you may have to tell someone and you don't know what will happen. Try to find out for your child what, if anything will happen.

➤ Don't urge the child to just try and forget about it - it may make the child feel as though it wasn't important, that they are not important and the way that they are feeling is not justified. If you find it difficult to speak with your child about what has happened contact someone or an agency that can help your child.

➤ Don't let the child believe that s/he caused any misery or pain within the family because s/he told someone about what was happening. Let your child know that it took a lot of strength and courage to tell someone and the way that you are feeling is not because of him/her.

➤ Do talk to a friend or family member you trust about how you are feeling. You and your feelings are important. Find out if anyone knows someone you can speak to about the abuse and your feelings.

Some Responses

of Parents

"I/We should have known!"

How could you have known? The child may have kept the abuse secret because s/he was too afraid to say. The child may have received threats from the abuser to stop her/him telling anyone. They may have been told it is their 'secret' (the abuser and child's'), that the abuser 'loves' them and won't 'love' them if they tell, that everyone will know, that it is normal, that they will break up the family if they tell. Abuse is always secret and abusers often use intimidation to keep it that way.

"I/We feel guilty/angry/upset/can't cope etc."

These are all understandable responses for parents. It is not you who is to blame. There is nothing you could have done to prevent the abuse. Speak to someone about the way you are feeling. You are good parents. You believe your child and that is what is important. You can cope. Find out what resources there are for you.

"It can't be true/ I don't believe this."

The initial shock of finding out may cause disbelief. How could this happen to my child? What have I done wrong? It costs nothing to believe. Why would a child lie about abuse? The biggest lie is when children say it doesn't happen at all when it has happened.

"What can I do?"

Listen to your child if s/he wants to talk. Believe what s/he is saying. Let the child know it wasn't his/her fault, that they didn't say or do anything, which made it happen, that they weren't to blame. If the child is old enough to make his/her own decisions let him/her make some choices e.g. who is going to be told about what has happened, would they like to speak to someone about it? Let the child know that you still love him/her, reassure the child that the way they are feeling is okay and understandable.

"My child is very young - how can I help her/him express her/his feelings?"

If a young child has been abused sometimes they can express themselves through drawing/painting/singing. For example "Let's draw a picture of .... Now what would you like to do with it, scribble him out, tear it up, throw it away?".

'I want to kill the ....'

It is wise to keep comments like this for other adults/friends. You could say, "I'm angry with the person who did this", "I'm upset but not with you". Children can feel responsible for the way their parents are feeling. They need reassurance, safety and love. Parents can help reassure their child by saying, "It's ok to cry, be sad, angry." Let them know it has happened to others and that they and the family can survive.

'It happened to me too when I was young'

This can be very difficult as it may reawaken long buried memories. Find someone to talk to about your own abuse. Helping yourself can make it easier to help your child in the longer term. Your child needs you to be strong for them so get help if you need to.

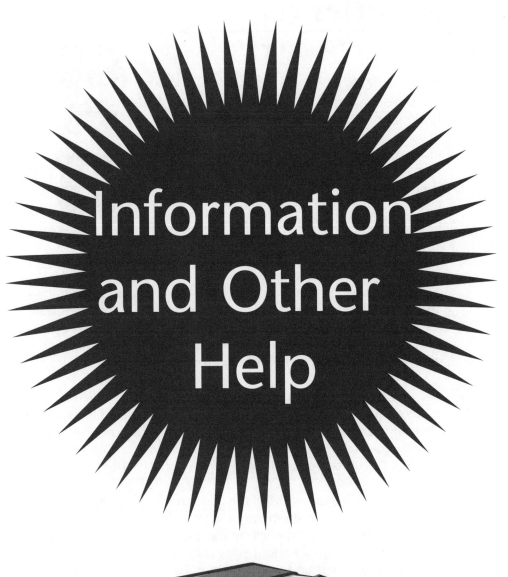

Information and Other Help

Agencies for
Young People

The Police

The police have a responsibility for prevention of crime as well as protection and investigation. While they can provide much needed help to a young survivor, there can be many barriers to a young person in approaching them for help. None of these barriers are insurmountable and a little bit of work on the part of adult supporters can make all the difference to breaking them down.

With younger children, we would hope that any adult who suspects abuse, or hears a disclosure, would act appropriately and inform police or social services, but with older young people, it is best to give them more control of the situation. Going over their heads often leads to a retraction and a breach of trust that often does not help them in the longer term.

Most police services now have specialised units, which exist to investigate allegations of child abuse, and the officers are generally very experienced in working with young people and very approachable. Usually they do not even wear a uniform and many of the units are not actually in the police station.

If you think that involving the police might be useful for the young person, talk to them about it and offer to make contact with the police on their behalf. In our experience the police are very open to being told about situations in a way that does not identify the survivor and will explain in detail how they would respond if the young person made a formal complaint. The police are also open to meeting the young person informally in a place of the young person's choosing and explaining the procedure in a non-threatening manner. All this can help break down the initial barriers to the young person speaking to the police.

Many young people view the police with suspicion and fear. Often their experience of the police has not been positive, and for those young survivors who have ever run away from home, the police have a responsibility for finding them and returning them. As the young person cannot tell about the true reason for running away, they are returned home to further abuse. It is understandable that these young people might not regard talking to the police as an option.

It can help a young survivor if you let them know that you or a person of their choice can remain with them throughout any procedures. Make sure, though, that you have agreed this with the police beforehand. You can let the young person know that they can stop at any time, can take a break and can leave when they want to. Often young people are so used to obeying the authority of adults that they need to be reminded that they can take some control. A young person is less likely to retract a statement if they are given the time and space to think, rather than being bulldozed into saying too much then taking fright or regretting it.

The Legal System

Unfortunately the legal system is not particularly friendly towards young people or survivors. More often than not, the young survivor feels that they are being failed and further abused by the processes they have to endure in going through the justice system. Few feel that they ever got justice at all. The better the young person is prepared for this, the better they will handle the outcomes in the end.

After giving a statement to the police, the police will seek other evidence in the form of interviewing any potential witnesses, asking for medical and other records to be released, interviewing and perhaps arresting the accused and asking the young person to consent to a medical examination. Usually the police inform the young person of all this before they begin to make a statement. If this has been over-looked, you as the supporter can find out the procedure and inform the young person.

After the police have finished their investigation into the allegation of abuse, they pass their findings to the appropriate body. In Scotland, this would be the Procurator Fiscal Office. It is this body, which decides whether or not, on the available evidence, to proceed with a case to court.

Sometimes there is insufficient evidence to proceed and the case may be passed to the social work department or Children's Hearing System (in Scotland). If there is enough evidence, then, after a lengthy period of time, which can in some cases be as much as two years, the case proceeds. If the accused has been held in prison on remand, the proceedings are much faster, but mostly the accused is not held awaiting trial, so it is best to let the young person know at the onset that it can take a long time to go to court.

Before the trial, the young survivor is summoned by the Prosecution to give a precognition statement. The defence agent also has the right to interview the complainer and other witnesses in the case. All this means that the young person may have to go through their side of the story at least three times before they actually appear in court to give evidence against the accused. The young person can be prepared for all of this with the help of an informed supporter. The young person can also make sure that they have a support person available, and that as far as possible they retain some control. The defence agent, for example, can talk to them at a place and time of the young person's choosing.

While there is some provision made for much younger children to give their evidence in court in a more protected way, i.e. with the use of video links or screens, older young people often have to face the accused without such protection. Either way is traumatic for a survivor of abuse. Things can be made a bit easier for the young person by preparing them for the trial. This might involve showing a young person round the courtroom before the trial, telling them who sits where, and what the procedures are, and making sure that they have support before, during and afterwards. Supporters would be well advised to make sure that they have with them a plentiful supply of such things as tissues, juice, sweets and something to distract the young survivor (books, games, personal stereo). They should also make sure that the young person has any medical aids that they may need with them such as an inhaler if they are asthmatic.

While it is never easy to appear as a witness in court against someone who has abused them, and the outcome of the case may seriously distress the young person, supporters who are well prepared can help reduce the stress considerably.

Often young people are distressed to find that before the trial begins or even halfway through, the accused has plea-bargained with the prosecution and a lesser charge than the original one has been accepted. In this, the accused pleads guilty to a lesser charge and the original charge is dropped. The survivor has no say in this and may be very angry and disappointed by this outcome.

The survivor of abuse has no one representing them in the court setting. As they are merely deemed to be a witness against the accused, they have no lawyer of their own. It is the Prosecutor who takes the case forward 'in the public interest', and no one person is appointed to act in the interests of the survivor. Many young people feel that this is wrong and become distressed by this. Again, if they are prepared for this, they can handle it all much better.

Social Work Department

When a case of child abuse comes to light, the social work department is often the first port of call for most people. In any investigations by the police, the investigation is carried out jointly with police and social work to reduce the amount of distress for the young person. Even if there is not enough evidence, social work will usually be informed that the young person has made a disclosure of abuse.

The social work department has a statutory duty to investigate child abuse, provide help for young people and can offer a range of services to young people and their families. Although there is an emphasis on trying to keep families together and supporting them in dealing with a variety of problems, social work must ensure that young people are not at risk. They do have the requirement to provide for young people who cannot or will not live at home. While it may be better to remove the abuser from the home situation, this may not always be possible and sometimes the young person has to be removed and cared for by the local authority. There are strict legal requirements that must be carried out before this happens.

Any young person at risk can demand from the social work department that they be offered a safe place to stay. If the young person can disclose the reason they are at risk and who from, then so much the better. Sometimes, though, for many of the reasons outlined in this book, young people just cannot tell what is happening to them. In this case, it is much more difficult for social work to respond. Supporters can suggest to the young person that disclosing even a little bit of information can help them stay safe. They do not have to do it all at once.

Health

Sometimes young survivors have health problems related to the abuse and would benefit greatly from seeking medical help. Many are very reluctant to do so and therefore suffer unnecessarily for long periods. It may be that the young person is so controlled by the abuser that the abuser does not permit them to see a doctor alone. Some doctors compound this by informing parents about visits from young people or refusing to see a young person alone. This only assists abusers and makes it more difficult for survivors to disclose.

Young people can be offered confidentiality if they are deemed to be able to understand enough. Doctors can decide this. They could also become more aware of issues of abuse and the many related health problems that can arise because of it. Not all abuse survivors will have obvious bruises that can be noticed. Not all young people asking for contraception are promiscuous! Some of them are trying to prevent pregnancy due to forced unwilling sex. Some young people presenting for abortions are pregnant as a result of abuse.

Supporters of young survivors can assist young people in accessing health services in a number of ways. They can find out what youth oriented services are in their area and what exactly they offer young people. They can offer to accompany young survivors to doctors. Alternatively they can offer to go and talk to the doctor on behalf of the young person and with the young person's consent.

Education

For some survivors of abuse, school is a safe place to be and education a welcome relief. Some throw themselves into education and become academic achievers. Others cannot concentrate enough to achieve much. Often, regardless of ability, young survivors of abuse miss out on a great deal of their education. They might be kept home by the abuser and prevented from going to school as another  means of exerting control over them. They may be kept off while injuries heal. They may suffer from recurring illness due to stress. They may truant for a variety of reasons. They may be excluded from school because of challenging behaviour.

No matter the reason for missing out on essential education, much can be done to address this. With the permission of the young survivor, teachers can be approached and told that there is a problem. Whereas it is preferable to be able to say what the problem is, teachers can be very understanding even if they are not told the whole reason. Teachers can also help a lot in providing additional academic help to assist the young survivor in catching up with the work. If they do not know that there is even a problem, it will be assumed that the young person is just being difficult or unreasonable. Rather than being regarded as a young person with problems, the young person can so easily be regarded as the problem.

Young people can be encouraged to consider going to college, as they get older so that they can get some qualifications. Supporters can help by finding out what is available in the way of suitable courses and what additional help can be provided to them in terms of learning support. Supporters can offer to help fill in forms and help to access courses.

Neighbourhood Resources

Most areas have a Community Centre offering a wide range of services to young people. This usually includes youth work and a Youth Information Service. These can be very valuable to young people as they are generally a good source of information and the youth workers are very skilled at working with and supporting young people. Many centres have groups and youth projects running and they can help young people to regain confidence and acquire new skills. These centres are very accessible to young people, and because they offer a general service, young people can feel more confident about no one knowing why they are going there.

Voluntary Organisations

There are many voluntary organisations that might also be able to help young survivors of abuse. Some provide short-term and long-term safe and supported accommodation and assist the young person in moving on towards independence. Others can provide counselling, befriending, advocacy and practical support. It is worth checking out what is available in your area as services vary widely.

Organisations such as rape crisis centres can provide support and some now cater for younger women. Women's Aid can often help if domestic violence is an issue and many now have children's workers. Childline offer a good telephone listening service across the country. Victim Support can often provide help, particularly in a court case, and larger organisations such as Barnardo's, Children First and NCH offer a wide range of services to families and young people.

Any one of these agencies would be able to put young people in touch with other services in their area.

Useful
Knowledge

Criminal Injuries Compensation

Any young survivor of abuse can apply for Criminal Injuries Compensation providing they have reported the abuse to the police and co-operated with the police and legal system. Even if the case does not go to court or the accused is found 'not guilty', they may still be entitled to receive this. An adult, usually the carer, can apply for this on behalf of the young survivor and if they get it, the money can be put in trust for the young person.

Victims of crime are compensated for the damages and injuries they suffered and although some immediate injuries might be obvious, with young survivors it is often difficult to know what the longer-term damage can turn out to be. Even though the young survivor may see the compensation in a negative light at first, it is still a good idea to apply for it as it may make a difference to them when they are older. The money can be used to pay for private therapy, a holiday away from the stress, or towards something that will help them recover from the abuse.

There is no guarantee that they will receive anything at all, and it is impossible to know if they are awarded compensation just how much they will receive.

Benefits

Young people who have been abused sometimes develop post-traumatic stress and become quite disabled for a while as a result of this. Many other things can also lead to a disability. Disability Living Allowance and Carers Allowance are two examples of benefits that these young people may be entitled to receive. Carers can apply on behalf of the young person and it is well worth checking out any entitlement to benefits.

Young people at the age of sixteen under special circumstances can claim Hardship Allowance and Housing Benefit; they may also qualify for a Community Care grant. It is always worth checking for the young person what is available to them.

Sometimes, young people find the whole benefits system very difficult to deal with and it can really help them if they have an informed adult support them through it. Even finding out for them what can be claimed is useful to them but many need the help of an adult to fill in the marathon forms. The benefits system is a myriad of confusion for young people and they are often so frustrated that they just give up trying. A supportive adult can make a tremendous difference in this area.

 ### Housing

Under 16's have no right to housing for themselves although there are safe houses in some parts of the country and social services  have a duty to attend to their accommodation needs. Unfortunately, if the young person cannot clearly say why they need alternative accommodation, they are very frequently taken home.

Young people aged 16, in Scotland at least, do have a right to access homeless accommodation. This isn't always as easy as it seems though. Many homeless units automatically contact parents and carers if a young person between 16 and 18 presents as homeless. For a young person fleeing from abuse, this is a disaster as the parent merely has to offer to take them back and they are no longer seen as homeless. Young people need to be very strong to stay put and insist on accommodation. Many flee as soon as the official reaches for the telephone.

Adult supporters can help by accompanying the young person and requesting the parents not be called. Supporters can also let the officials know as much about the abuse as the young person permits. It is important to talk this through with the young person beforehand so that you know how much the young person is comfortable with revealing. Housing workers are becoming much more aware of abuse now so it can often be enough for an adult supporter to say that there is a very good reason for not calling the parents.

Most young people who have been abused benefit most from supported accommodation. Unfortunately there is still quite a dearth of this accommodation. Supporters can find out what is available in other areas besides there own geographical area. Many young survivors are, in any case, too afraid to stay in the same town as their abusers and therefore keen to move away.

Young people in very difficult circumstances who cannot as yet disclose the abuse can present at social services and demand to be looked after. If they refuse to give their name or any other details at all and are clearly under age, they must be looked after until their identities can be discovered. By then, hopefully they will have built a relationship with a worker enough so that they can then disclose enough to be kept safe.

Resources
and
Exercises

Introduction

This section of the book has suggestions, worksheets and exercises that workers can use with a young person to help them explore any issues they may have. Some young people will welcome activities such as these while others will simply not engage with you at all in this manner.

Sometimes having exercises to work through are a great practical help to both the worker and the young person but it should always be done by mutual arrangement. There is little to be gained from forcing a young survivor to do work. They may not be ready for it and working through problems is best done with the full cooperation of the young survivor.

It is important to bear in mind with any work that you do with a young survivor that many young people cannot read very well. Even a teenager may not be a competent reader and they may not want you to know that their reading skills are not very good and may express disinterest rather than admit that they cannot read.

The other thing to bear in mind is that not all survivors are the same. Just because something works well for one survivor does not mean that it can then be applied to others in exactly the same way. It is best to be adaptable and resourceful in your approach.

The exercises are there as a resource which can be adapted to suit the different needs of different young people. Some young people may find that writing works for them, others may use drawing and some may use neither. You can adapt games and make use of toys, music, poetry, pottery, craftwork and anything else you can think of to help a young survivor explore their feelings.

We have successfully used balloons on occasions to represent the abuser and help young people with no speech to express their feelings of rage and anger. We have also used trips to the bottle bank for a glass smashing session (be careful of the glass), building sand castles and drawing stories in the sand, kicking autumn leaves and smashing winter ice on the pond to express many thoughts and feelings.

We have also successfully used dartboards, drums, collages and paper mache in a variety of ways to help the young person explore safe ways of letting out anger. There need be no limit to young imaginations or yours in finding creative ways of exploring issues and feelings about abuse.

Practical

Support

It is not possible for a support worker to be there 24 hours a day for someone. So one thing you need to take a look at is ways for the survivor to deal with feelings and memories when they come up. The following are a few ideas, suggestions you can give to try and help a survivor express themselves.

Writing: A note pad and pen can be there 24 hours a day! Writing down things like memories, feelings, bad dreams, how he or she feels about the abuser and what they want to talk about at the next meeting with you.

Drawing: Some young survivors may feel happier about using drawing or painting to express themselves - this can be therapeutic in itself. The survivor holds onto the power and can destroy the work, post it to their support worker or do with it as they please. They have the control over the work they do.

Writing lists: Making lists can be very useful. The following are list headings, which survivors can try out. 'Things I can do when I'm feeling sad.' 'Things I can do when I'm feeling suicidal.' 'Things I can do when I'm feeling angry.' Encourage the survivor to write lists such as these. Sometimes when survivors become overwhelmed with a feeling they can't think about what they can do to change it, having a list means they can look back and say, "I'll try this. If that doesn't work I'll try the next thing on my list." The list can have things on it such as, hugging the teddy bear, doing some relaxation exercises, phoning my best friend, going for a walk and phoning Childline.

Support work is about listening to the survivor, believing them, helping them express how they feel and exploring the reasons behind how they are feeling. The following exercises are exercises for dealing with specific feelings. You cannot, and should not try to force a survivor to do what you want. You can only make suggestions about what they could try, which may help.

Anger: We are brought up not to express our anger. This is particularly true of young women. Often others don't like it, don't know how to deal with it and don't approve of it. Anger, like any other feeling, needs to be safely expressed. The following are ideas of how to help a young survivor express their anger in a positive manner.

➢ Punching a mattress, pillow or cushion until exhausted.

➢ Get some eggs, draw faces on them and/or write names on them and then smash them on walls or floors (Don't forget to clean up afterwards!)

➢ Get some balloons, draw faces on them, name them and then burst them.

➢ Write a list, "What I would like to do to my abuser/abusers".

➢ In the bath, using bubble bath, build a bubble man then destroy it, watch it go down the plughole afterwards.

➢ Get some soap crayons, graffiti the tiles in your bathroom (It'll clean up easily after.)

➢ Go to a gym that has a punch bag.

➢ Write or draw what has happened to make you angry, who has made you angry and how you feel.

Sad and suicidal

> Talk to someone you trust.

> Have a list prepared, "people I can contact when I'm feeling down" work through this list. You can also go through the list "Things I can do when I'm feeling sad."

> Write down the reasons you are feeling sad or suicidal.

> Get a close friend / support worker to write down a list of your positive qualities. Read through this. (This can be done as an exercise with the supporter/survivor; get the survivor to write a list on how she sees herself, while you write a list of how you see the survivor, compare the two. The survivor quite often cannot think of positive ways to describe her/himself. This is their view of themselves. Show them your list of the positive qualities that the survivor has. This should include courage and strength as it takes courage and strength to speak out about abuse.

Guilt: A great many young survivors believe that they have done something to cause the abuse, or they should have done something to stop the abuse. This can cause feelings of guilt, blame or shame.

> Suggest that the survivor to write a list *"I feel guilty, because.... I feel I am to blame, because...... I feel ashamed, because......"* See what is brought up and gently challenge their beliefs, if appropriate.

> Encourage the survivor to think about who had the power and who didn't.

> Think about who made the decisions in the abusive situation.

Play: Don't forget the value of play in helping young survivors to talk and heal. Play Mobil figures, plasticine, dolls and a wide variety of toys can be used to represent people, situations, feelings and events and can take the edge off directly talking about things. Many young people are embarrassed about talking about the abuse and prefer to talk indirectly though play figures.

The above are just a few ideas of work, which a survivor can do for her or himself or with the help of a support worker. These are by no means all the ways of dealing with a vast range of feelings but are basic ways of helping the survivor to help themselves. If you are ever unsure about whether something is suitable - don't use it.

Don't be afraid to ask others for help.

Remember this is the young person's life and try not to get too involved or over anxious in your keenness to help them through it. Sometimes all that a young survivor needs is to know that you are there for them and that you care about them.

Problem
Solving

All of us at some time in our lives have been faced with problems and had to find a way of dealing with them. There are many different ways of tackling problems and we have probably all, through our life experiences, developed strategies for resolving problems.

Younger people do not have the advantage of life experience and can sometimes drift from crisis to crisis without developing a way of solving the many problems, which can arise for them. While it may not be your job to teach problem solving techniques, sometimes it will be appropriate to help the young person look more closely at ways of resolving a difficult situation. You can draw on your own experience in this and share with the young survivor ways in which you have resolved problems (remember to keep your own problems out).

Here is one example of a problem solving technique.

START & ENABLE

For the person with the problem:

Speak - speaking over the problem with someone is an important first step in resolving a problem.

Many young people keep their problems to themselves or act them out in their behaviour. There are many reasons for young people finding it difficult to speak, especially about abuse. These include such things as fear of the consequences, fear of the abuser and no one they can trust to tell it to.

It is important to try to encourage the young person to talk about things. Sometimes just speaking about it can really help.

Think - thinking over the issues can help clarify the problem. Encourage the young person to take the time to think things over. You can suggest ways of clarifying thoughts and coming up with ideas, for example:

→ Writing it down.

→ Making lists of pros and cons

→ Drawing pictures

→ Using toys or objects to represent the problems

→ Making up a story or play with a different ending

→ Brainstorming

Act - making clear decisions, which can be acted on to try to resolve the problem.

Helping the person find direction and perhaps making an action plan looking at.

The *long-term* goal: i.e. the desired outcome. Try to ensure that it is an achievable goal and there is a realistic timescale.

The *short-term* goal: i.e. small steps forward that can be achieved quickly and easily.

Review - going back over the problem to see how things have developed. Encourage them to review the situation at intervals. Suggestions of keeping a diary, making notes etc., can help them see just how far they've come.

Treat - Encourage them to reward their own efforts and stop and treat themselves occasionally. This can be a great confidence builder and anyway we all deserve occasional treats.

For the supporter:

Empathise - try to put yourself in the young person's shoes and try to understand.

Nurture - show you care for the young person, praise all efforts and be with the young person.

Attitude - be non- judgemental, non-directive, non-patronising and above all human.

Believe - believe in the young person and what she or he is trying to tell you.

Listen - listen to what the young person says, and doesn't say, notice the body language. Listen with your eyes as well as your ears.

Encourage - encourage the young person to take charge of his or her life, to speak out and survive.

This sheet is useful for helping young people look at telling about the abuse. Sometimes they get so caught up in the aftermath of disclosure that they lose sight of the original and valid reasons for telling.

Why I Told...

Things That Have Changed Because I Told...

Anger: Some young survivors confuse anger and violence and this sheet can be used to help them clarify the differences.

When My Mother gets Angry She...

_____
_____
_____

When My Father Gets Angry He...

_____
_____
_____

When I Get Angry I...

_____
_____
_____

When Someone Gets Angry with me, I...

_____
_____
_____

I'm Angry at...

_____
_____

Because...

_____
_____
_____

What do Angry People Do?

_____

_____

_____

What do Violent people Do?

_____

_____

_____

Can I Imagine Anger that Is not Violent?

Please tick ✔

Yes ☐   No ☐   Don't Know ☐

Write a list of non-violent things you could try when angry.

When I get angry I could....

1. _____

2. _____

3. _____

4. _____

5 _____

Draw your angry feelings!

This worksheet is useful for helping young people explore the differences between fantasy and reality. Some young survivors take refuge in a fantasy world and need help to sort this out for themselves.

Fantasy and Reality

I wish that I ...

_____

_____

_____

Go back over your list. Which could really happen... ?

_____

_____

_____

Which are unlikely to happen...?

_____

_____

_____

Which ones are impossible...?

_____

_____

_____

Draw something real that you would like.

Me: This worksheet is good for exploring how the young survivor perceives self. Often survivors find it difficult to find things they like about themselves and need help to see their good qualities.

The things I like About Me Are...

_____

_____

_____

The Things I Don't like about Me Are...

_____

_____

_____

The Things I Want to Change About me Are...

_____

_____

_____

The Things I Can Really Change About Me Are...

_____

_____

_____

The Things I'm Good at Are....

_____

_____

_____

Feelings: This worksheet is useful for exploring where the young person is at in their views of themselves. It can be useful to do this worksheet at the beginning of support and then do it again after working with the young survivor for a few months to see what, if any changes have happened.

How Do I Feel? Please tick ✔

	Always	Usually	Sometimes	Never
I feel dirty	❏	❏	❏	❏
I think I'm crazy	❏	❏	❏	❏
I feel ashamed	❏	❏	❏	❏
I'm different	❏	❏	❏	❏
I feel powerless	❏	❏	❏	❏
I want to die	❏	❏	❏	❏
I hate myself	❏	❏	❏	❏
I'm confused	❏	❏	❏	❏
I'm scared	❏	❏	❏	❏
I shoplift	❏	❏	❏	❏
I feel alone	❏	❏	❏	❏
I am stupid	❏	❏	❏	❏
No one cares	❏	❏	❏	❏
I feel to blame	❏	❏	❏	❏
No one likes me	❏	❏	❏	❏
I feel scared	❏	❏	❏	❏

Strengths: Many young survivors have such low self-esteem that they find it difficult to see their own strengths. You can help them work through the following.

What Are Your Strengths?
(If you're not sure ask a friend what they think!)

Have you survived?

Do you have courage?

Are you determined?

Are you a caring person?

Are you a good listener?

Are you independent?

Can you handle a crisis?

Are you clever?

Are you calm and patient?

Are you hard working?

Do you have empathy and understanding?

Do you ever help others?

Are you a fighter?

Are you unique?

What else are you?

Sex: Some young survivors find great difficulty in sexual relationships and this sheet can be useful for helping them set their own boundaries and stay in control. This worksheet is best done with both partners.

Ground Rules for Sex

What rules or limits would I like to set?

_____

_____

_____

Things that make me feel good are....

_____

_____

_____

Things that make me feel bad are....

_____

_____

_____

Under what conditions will I be sexual?

_____

_____

_____

Sex would be better if..........

_____

_____

_____

Things that would help me feel safer with sex are......

_____

_____

_____

Goals: This worksheet can help young people to look at taking charge of their lives and setting their own goals. Try to assist them in keeping the goals realistic and achievable.

One-Month Goals

My goals this month are......

_____

_____

_____

_____

Barriers to this are.....

_____

_____

_____

_____

Actions that might raise the barriers are......

_____

_____

_____

_____

I will begin by......

_____

_____

_____

_____

_____

_____

_____

I will get help and support from.....

_____

_____

_____

_____

I will know I have achieved my goal by..

_____

_____

_____

_____

_____

Self Injury Prevention Plan

When I feel like injuring myself I will

_____

_____

_____

_____

_____

I will not

_____

_____

_____

_____

_____

I will telephone _____ on _____

If I can't get through, I will call _____ on _____

I deserve not to hurt because

_____

_____

_____

_____

_____

_____

_____

Before I do anything that will injure myself I will work through my personal list right to the end.

Signed_____ date ____/__ / ___

Personal List for Prevention of Self Injury

1. Concentrate on breathing; focus on getting grounded and feeling at peace with self.

2. _____

_____

3. _____

_____

4. _____

5. _____

_____

_____

6. _____

_____

7. _____

_____

8. _____

_____

9. _____

_____

10. Go back to one and work through the list again.

Self-Injury Worksheet

Before I harm myself I usually feel ....

_____

_____

_____

_____

_____

_____

After I harm myself, I usually feel.....

_____

_____

_____

_____

_____

_____

Instead of self-injury I can try....

_____

_____

_____

_____

_____

Other Titles by
Vip Publications

Subject	Title	Price		Postage
■ **Abuse**	**Teen Vip Training Pack:**	£55.00	plus	£5.00 p&p
Prevention	**Jenny's Story**	£6.50	plus	£0.50 p&p
	Wee Vip Pack: Game, Story, Video.	£95.00	plus	£5.00 p&p
	Jonny Cool: Storybook	£10.00	plus	£1.50 p&p
	Jonny Cool: Workbook	£5.00	plus	£1.50 p&p
	Jonny Cool: Workbook & Storybook	£15.00	plus	£5.00 p&p
■ **Games**	**Truth! Dare! Scare!:** Safety Game	£55.00	plus	£5.00 p&p
■ **Poetry Books**	**Hear We are again**	£3.50	plus	£0.50 p&p
	Listen! Hear!	£3.50	plus	£0.50 p&p
	Hear! We are!	£3.50	plus	£0.50 p&p
	Hear! Us!	£3.50	plus	£0.50 p&p
■ **StoryTime Series**	1,2 or 3	£5.00 ea.	plus	£1.50 p&p
	Books			
■ **Music**	**After the Storm** CD	£10.00	plus	£5.00 p&p
	After the Storm T-shirt	£6.50	plus	£1.50 p&p
■ **Information**	**Postcards** (8)	£3.50	plus	£0.50 p&p
	Information Booklets	Free	plus	£0.50 p&p
■ **Books**	**Who Dares Wins!**	£15.00	plus	£5.00 p&p
	Ritual Abuse book			

All these publications are available from:
Young Women's Centre,
1 Victoria Road, Dundee, DD1 1EL
Telephone: 01382 206 222

Please make cheques payable to "Dundee Young Women's Centre (Trading) Ltd"
Please enclose remittance to the value of the cover price plus the cost shown for postage
and packing. Applicable only in the UK. Overseas prices on application. Prices are subject
to change without notice.